D1448693

THE ECONOMICS OF INFLATION

SAMUEL A. MORLEY
The University of Wisconsin

THE DRYDEN PRESS INC.
Hinsdale, Illinois

For Monica

PRINTED WITH RECYCLED PAPER

Copyright © 1971 by The Dryden Press Inc.

All rights reserved
Library of Congress Catalog Card Number: 72–116112
ISBN: 0–03–089097–7

Printed in the United States of America
4 3 2 1   008   1 2 3 4 5 6 7 8 9

PREFACE

This book develops a simple model of the inflationary process for use in any undergraduate macroeconomics course. It was written specifically for use in the second half of a one-semester introductory course and presupposes knowledge of a basic model of income determination.

The literature on inflation is vast, and I do not attempt to summarize it in this book. Rather I develop what I hope is the simplifying central theme which ties together many different current theories of inflation. There are two leading explanations or analyses of inflation. The quantity theory, one major analysis, relates changes in money income to changes in money supply. This theory, however, has never been very clear about how the changes in money income are divided between changes in output and changes in prices. The presupposition has been that all the change comes in prices, none in output.

The Phillips curve, the second main analysis of inflation, centers around the relation between inflation and output or unemployment. The Phillips curve is concerned with exactly that question slurred over by the traditional quantity theory— how changes in money income become translated into quantity and price changes.

Recent work, using dynamic models of the inflationary process, is linking the two theories. This book is an example of such an approach, and like most of the other models of inflation it stresses expectations. It focuses on expectations by labor, assuming that labor sometimes makes erroneous forecasts of the current price level. It then shows how and why an exogenous increase in demand generates a typical cycle of rising output and employment, followed by rising wages and prices. If a government attempts to stabilize, output and employment decline although prices and wages continue to rise. The first part of this process used to be called demand-pull inflation; the second, cost-push inflation. But if our model of price expectations is applicable, we should regard both demand pull and cost push as connected parts of a single inflationary price.

Thus the recent expectations models of the inflationary process predict what could be called a short-run relation between inflation and output or unemployment whenever expected prices are not equal to actual prices. They provide a prediction of how the quantity theory increase in money income is split into price and output changes. But this is not permanent, because the forecasting errors causing it must eventually be corrected. In the long run, expected and actual prices must be equal. When they are, the economy returns to the quantity theory world, where changes in nominal income cause changes only in prices, not in employment or output.

I depend heavily on expectations by labor in this book. This allows the combining of the traditional quantity theory explanation of inflation and the more recent emphasis on the Phillips curve. But more important, it encourages the consideration of inflation as the dynamic process by which an economy reacts to excess demand over time. The process has certain characteristic phases and features that must be recognized if we are to understand the troublesome problem of stabilization and the true nature of the trade-off between inflation and unemployment.

My intellectual and personal debts in writing this book are many. Donald Nichols deserves my special thanks for his insights and encouragement. I am grateful to Stephen Welch, Eugene Smolensky, Milton Friedman, Donald Hester, Allen Kelley, Albert Fishlow, Antonio Delfim Neto, and Phillip Robins for comments on the text and ideas on inflation which have profoundly influenced my approach to the problem. My thanks also to the students in my Introductory Economics class, who served willingly and patiently as guinea pigs while I developed this material. For her efforts to transform my economics jargon into readable English I thank Sara Boyajian. Finally, my thanks to Chris Schultz for the interest, care, and perseverance with which she readied this manuscript for publication.

Madison, Wisconsin   S. A. M.
August 1971

CONTENTS

Preface   iii

Chapter 1   Theories of Inflation   1
            The Phillips Curve   3
            Overview of the Argument Presented in This
                Book   4
            Method of Analysis   6

Chapter 2   Inflation: Measurement and Costs   8
            A Definition of Inflation   8
            Measurement of Inflation   9
            What Price Indices Are   12
            Difference between Nominal and Deflated
                Magnitudes   13
            Costs of Inflation   15
            Inflation and Labor   16
            Expected Inflation and Financial Markets   18

Chapter 3   Inflation and the Labor Market   23
            Demand for Labor   23
            Supply of Labor   26
            Determination of Equilibrium Employment and
                Wages   31
            Effect of Unexpected Inflation on
                Employment   34
            Effect of Expected Inflation on the Labor
                Market   40
            Formation of Expectations   41

Chapter 4   Inflation and the Goods Market   46
            Supply and Demand for Individual
               Commodities   46
            Aggregate Demand and Supply   47
            Effect of Inflation on Aggregate Supply   50
            Goods Market Equilibrium   54
            Is There a Trade-off between Inflation and
               Output?   54
            Cost-Push and Demand-Pull Inflation   57

Chapter 5   A Description of the Inflationary Process   65
            Adjustment to Excess Demand with No
               Expected Inflation   65
            Effect of Expected Inflation on the Adjustment
               Process   74
            Comparison of the Hypothetical Inflation Proc-
               ess and Actual Inflations   78
            The Trade-off between Output and
               Employment   83

Chapter 6   The Phillips Curve   89
            Phillips Curve as a Result of Erroneous Price
               Forecasts   91
            Short-Run versus Long-Run Phillips
               Curves   101
            Stabilization Paths   102

Chapter 7   Inflation and the Distribution of Income   111
            Effect of Inflation on Income of the Poor   111
            Inflation and the Uses of Income   119
            Inflation and Wealth   120
            Inflation, Factor Returns, and the Functional
               Distribution of Income   121

Chapter 8   The Problem of Stabilization   129
            Gradual versus Rapid Stabilization   131
            Monetary versus Fiscal Policy   132
            Wage and Price Controls or Guideposts   137

Appendix 1 Tables   142

Appendix 2 Readings on Inflation and Development   151

THE ECONOMICS
OF INFLATION

1
CHAPTER

Theories
of Inflation

Prior to 1940 most economists held the opinion that all inflations were caused by excess demand generated by expansions in the money supply. Economic history seems to favor this simple explanation. A recently published price series for England allows us to review inflation since medieval times.[1] Three major periods of unreversed increases in prices—inflation—can be distinguished, each associated with a large increase in the money supply. The first occurred from 1525 to 1650, when the Spanish discovered gold in the New World. The second occurred in the second half of the eighteenth century, at the time of the invention of fractional reserve banking and the resultant expansion of bank or credit money. The last period ran from 1932 to 1959, when governments discovered deficit financing and the world was engaged in war.

The association of rising prices with monetary growth was formalized in the quantity theory, whose most recent and sophisticated advocate is Milton Friedman. The quantity theor-

---

[1] R. G. Lipsey, "Does Money Always Depreciate?" *Lloyd's Bank Review* (October 1960), pp. 1–13.

ists assert that no inflation is possible without an expansion in the money supply, that all inflations are caused by excess demand, and that a critical element in controlling inflation is stopping the expansion of money. Presumably the mechanism by which higher prices follow from an increase in the money supply is a straightforward application of monetary theory. An increase in the money supply leads to a decrease in the interest rate, thus encouraging investment in consumer and producer durables. This increases aggregate demand, leading to increases in output, in higher prices, or in both output and higher prices, depending on whether or not the economy is at full employment. Such inflations should be accompanied by full employment and full use of capacity. Neither men nor machines should be idle.

After the Korean War, however, the United States appeared to have entered a different inflationary phase. Prices rose, despite substantial unemployment. Some observers believed that strong labor unions were forcing business to raise its prices to cover costs. Economists invented the term "cost-push inflation" to describe this phenomenon. The distinguishing feature of cost-push inflation is rising wages with high rates of unemployment and constant or even declining output. Obviously, by itself, a rise in wages is not sufficient to label an inflation cost push, because rising wages would also be expected to occur in the typical excess demand situation (along with full employment and a high level of output).

During the 1950s economists tended to analyze inflations by classifying them as either cost push or demand pull, as the excess-demand, full-employment inflation came to be called. Yet there are problems associated with this classification scheme. One difficulty in labeling a particular inflation as either cost push or demand pull is that the classification depends on the starting point. This year's wage increases may be the result of last year's price increases. Labor may be trying to catch up with an unexpected rise in the cost of living, so that the cause of the latter may also be the cause of the former. If one ignores previous years, he will call this year's wage increases evidence of cost-push inflation. But what if those wage boosts are really a delayed reaction to prior inflation? Then all the years are part of a single inflationary process, and it makes no sense to classify separately the causes of increasing prices in any particular year.

A modern view of inflation tends to ignore the distinction between cost push and demand pull and to think of inflation as a process with certain characteristic phases. Typically the initial phase, which we call the expansionary phase, will show all the symptoms of demand-pull inflation. Wages are rising, and output and employment are high and probably growing. At some point the economy enters a second phase, in which output and employment level off or fall. But prices and wages still rise, with wages generally rising faster than prices; this phase was called cost-push inflation. We could label it the stabilization phase of the inflationary process, and it is part of the adjustment by the economy to previous excess demand.

Following this interpretation one could think of the cost-push inflation of the 1950s as the stabilization phase of an inflationary process that began with World War II. That phase was completed by around 1960, when a new expansion began. The early 1970s now appear to be the stabilization phase of an inflation that began about 1965 with the expenditures on the war in Vietnam.

One of the principal purposes of this book is to develop a simple economic framework that will generate this two-phase inflationary process. It offers one possible explanation of how the process works and what roles excess demand for goods and labor's wage demands play. With it the reader should gain some perspective on the difficult process of stabilization that the United States will be encountering in the early 1970s.

The Phillips Curve

In 1958, A. W. Phillips published an article in which he showed that an observable relation existed between the rate of change in wages and the level of unemployment for the United Kingdom. This relation, known as the Phillips curve, was later verified for the United States and extended to the rate of change in prices. We will investigate the Phillips curve in detail in Chapter 6. It will suffice here to state that the Phillips curve suggests that wage or price increases lower the level of unemployment, or, to put it more precisely, that the policies leading to inflation also lead to low levels of unemployment. If this relation between unemployment and inflation is stable, it would have the far-reaching implication that there is a trade-off between rising prices and unemployment. A country could choose a low rate of unemployment at the cost of a relatively high rate of inflation or vice versa.

Recent writing has begun to cast doubt on the validity of the trade-off between inflation and unemployment. Economists, such as Milton Friedman and Edmund Phelps, assert that the relation results from erroneous expectations about inflation. Increasing prices raise employment and output in the short run, so long as labor is surprised by the inflation. When labor reacts to the loss of purchasing power it has suffered because of unexpected inflation, the whole process is reversed. Wages rise and employment and output fall. In the long run there is no trade-off between inflation and employment; output and employment are independent of the level of prices.

Overview of the Argument Presented in This Book

We are going to develop a model which shows how the inflationary process works. The process is one during which prices, wages, and expectations all change in certain predictable ways. The analysis is intended to illuminate two central issues in inflation theory; namely: Is the cause of inflation demand pull or cost push? Is the supposed trade-off between inflation and unemployment illustrated by the Phillips curve a valid one for policy makers?

Central to our analysis is the role of price expectations by labor. We assume that labor reacts to price changes with a lag. This means that in the short run an inflation can reduce the real cost of labor. If a worker does not adjust his wages as prices rise, the employer will find that hiring additional workers is profitable. Rising prices will increase employment and output when the actual rate of inflation is greater than that expected by labor. When labor belatedly realizes what has occurred, and reacts to its loss of purchasing power, the process

4

is reversed; wages and prices rise while output and employment fall.

I have labeled the first phase of inflation the expansion phase. In this phase actual rates of inflation are greater than those expected by labor. Inflation takes labor by surprise, and output and employment rise. The expansion phase is what used to be called demand-pull inflation.

The second phase of the inflationary process, where labor demands wage increases to make up for past unexpected inflation, I have called the stabilization phase. This is the phase that has been labeled cost-push inflation. Typically, during this phase, output and employment are falling as the government acts to control demand, but prices and wages continue to rise.

In my view both phases should be viewed as connected parts of a single inflationary process. The expansion phase takes place while the perception of inflation by labor lags; the stabilization phase occurs when labor expectations about inflation adjust to the new realities. We thus conclude that the dichotomy between cost push and demand pull is a false one, because both types are predictable parts of a single inflationary process.

The model presented here is also relevant to the Phillips curve controversy over the meaning and stability of the observed relation between inflation and unemployment. We will see that such a relation is implied by the model, *but* it is a short-run relation resulting from erroneous expectations about inflation. As we have already suggested, when labor incorrectly forecasts prices or reacts to inflation with a lag, inflation can increase employment and output. During the expansion phase, inflation occurs with falling unemployment and rising output, precisely the Phillips curve relation. Thus, in our view, the Phillips curve relation is just another way of representing the process by which an economy reacts to variations in demand.

The stabilization phase is not so simple. In this phase, labor is attempting to adjust its expectations to previous inflation. We shall show that in this situation the economy moves from one Phillips curve to another. This is what causes the uncomfortable combination of continued inflation and rising unemployment.

Thus one could think of the Phillips curve as a short-run

5

relation arising from erroneous price expectations by labor. As labor corrects these inflation forecasts, the short-run curve shifts and the supposed trade-off between inflation and unemployment disappears.

Method of Analysis

The preceding section has laid out our entire model of how the inflationary process works. Before embarking on the analysis that leads to those results, it is useful to say a word about the method we are going to use. The method must be dynamic for inflation is a dynamic process. In this type of analysis we are seeking a path, not a point. This differs from the usual procedure in macroeconomics. Generally we study problems like the determination of income. We find the level of income at a point, which would be equivalent to finding the level of prices at a point. That is an equilibrium analysis, the study of the characteristics of a position at which an economy will come to rest. By contrast, inflation analysis is a disequilibrium, or dynamic, analysis. It studies the process by which prices and other variables move over time, perhaps as the economy moves from one equilibrium to another.

In order to make dynamic analysis easier, economists have adopted a convention. They artificially break up time into periods and study the determination of prices (when studying inflation) during each period. When they put the periods together, they have a price path. It is somewhat like making a movie by pasting together a set of still pictures.

In studying inflation we are going to make use of this period analysis, so our problem will be to understand how prices, output, and employment are determined during each period and how the current period is influenced by the past and by expectations about the future. Our hope is that by thinking of inflation as a disequilibrium adjustment process with prices, wages, and expectations all interacting over time, we can get a more sophisticated viewpoint on such matters as the cause of inflation, the inflation-output trade-off, and the stabilization process.

Questions

1. Exactly what is inflation? Why should we be concerned with it?
2. What groups would you expect to be hurt by an inflation? to be helped by it?

Suggestions for Further Reading

Bronfenbrenner, Martin, and F. D. Holzman, "Survey of Inflation Theory," *American Economic Review* (September 1963), 593–661.

Brown, A. J., *The Great Inflation, 1939–1951*. London: Oxford University Press, 1955.

Friedman, Milton, *Dollars and Deficits*, Chapters 1, 3. Englewood Cliffs, N. J.: Prentice-Hall, 1968.

Johnson, Harry G., "A Survey of Theories of Inflation," in H. G. Johnson, *Essays in Monetary Economics*. Cambridge, Mass.: Harvard University Press, 1967.

Lipsey, Richard, "Does Money Always Depreciate?" *Lloyd's Bank Review* (October 1960), 1–13.

General Introductory Source Books in Inflation

Ball, R. J., and Peter Doyle, eds., *Inflation*. Baltimore, Md.: Penguin, 1969.

Perlman, Richard, ed., *Inflation: Demand Pull or Cost Push*. Boston: D. C. Heath, 1965.

2

CHAPTER

Inflation:
Measurement
and Costs

Before discussing the causes of inflation and the dilemmas it poses for policy makers, it is useful to take a closer look at what inflation is, how it can be measured, and why it is considered undesirable.

A Definition of Inflation

What is inflation? The immediate response is, rising prices —the working definition we will use in this book. But we can go one step further and ask, what causes those rising prices? This may appear to be an unanswerable question; we are going to argue, however, that rising prices are always caused by excess demand, meaning that buyers would like to buy more than sellers are willing to sell. But, you must be saying, at what prices? There is always excess demand at some set of prices. If the price of Chevrolets falls low enough, eventually the number of buyers will be greater than the number of cars that General Motors is willing to produce. So let us be more precise and say that inflation occurs whenever there is excess demand at last year's prices. That is, buyers would like to buy

8

more than sellers are willing to sell at last year's prices. In such a situation prices will rise from last year's level to a point where buyers and sellers are agreed on a single quantity that is to be willingly produced and purchased. Whenever there is excess demand, as we have defined it, prices will be rising. Rising prices—inflation—are the symptom of excess demand. With price controls the causal link between excess demand and inflation is broken. Rising prices are replaced by rationing or waiting in lines. Under these circumstances one can learn little by studying the behavior of prices.

Measurement of Inflation

We have been speaking rather glibly about price increases and rates of inflation without worrying too much about measurement. Yet the measurement of rising prices is not simple in a complex economy that produces and consumes many different goods. For a single commodity, we can collect a historical series of prices, and from it can calculate the rate of change in the price of the commodity. If there were only one commodity in the economy, the change in its price would be the rate of inflation. But when many commodities exist, each commodity may have a different rate of price change, and we must find some way of averaging them.

The way we add the various rates of price change to create an aggregate rate of inflation depends on what we wish to use that information for. If we wish to measure the rate at which the cost of living has increased, we will do it differently depending on whose cost of living is being studied. Clearly the cost of living to an upper income suburbanite varies with the price of automobiles, lawn fertilizer, and butter. To a ghetto dweller, the cost of buses and subways, rat poison, and margarine may be more important. For each family we are concerned with how the increase in prices has affected its ability to buy commodities. Therefore we need include only those price changes relevant to the family in question, and average them in a manner that reflects their importance.

In a multicommodity world we aggregate by constructing a weighted average of individual price changes. We do so by multiplying each percentage change by the share of its commodity in the consumer budget. For example, consider the following hypothetical consumption price scheme (Table 2.1).

TABLE 2.1

Consumption in a Simple Economy

Commodity	Price	Quantity Produced	Sales
		1970	
Cars	$2,000	100	$ 200,000
Bread	0.50	1,000,000	500,000
Oranges	0.30	1,000,000	300,000
Total Consumption			$1,000,000
		1971	
Cars	$2,500	110	$ 275,000
Bread	0.60	1,100,000	660,000
Oranges	0.30	1,100,000	330,000
Total Consumption			$1,265,000

Cars make up 20 percent of total consumption; bread, 50 percent; and oranges, 30 percent. We can therefore calculate the change in the cost of living by the following weighted average:

Change in Cost of Living

Commodity	Change in Price		Share		
Cars	(0.25)	$\times$	0.2	$=$	0.05
Bread	(0.20)	$\times$	0.5	$=$	+0.10
Oranges	0	$\times$	0.3	$=$	+0
					0.15

10

On average, prices have risen by 15 percent during 1970 in the example. Notice that this does not represent the price behavior of any individual commodity.

What does this 15 percent rate of inflation indicate? It indicates at a glance how much more money is required in 1971 to buy the 1970 bundle of goods. If we multiply the 1970 quantities from Table 2.1 by the 1971 prices, we find that the total dollar expenditure is exactly 15 percent higher.

Commodity	1971 Prices	×	1970 Output	=	Money Value of 1970 Consumption in 1971 Prices
Cars	2,500	×	100	=	$ 250,000
+ Bread	0.60	×	1,000,000	=	600,000
+ Oranges	0.30	×	1,000,000	=	300,000
					$1,150,000

It costs $1.150 million, or 15 percent more, in 1971 to purchase the same amount of goods that could have been purchased for $1 million in 1970.[1]

---

[1] The change in the cost of living can be constructed by dividing either a weighted average of the individual rates of inflation or the ratio of 1971 quantities valued at 1970 prices by 1970 quantities at 1970 prices minus one. The two methods are algebraically equivalent.

$$\text{Inflation} = \frac{P_c^{71}Q_c^{70} + P_b^{71}Q_b^{70} + P_o^{71}Q_o^{70} - P_c^{70}Q_c^{70} - P_b^{70}Q_b^{70} - P_o^{70}Q_o^{70}}{(P_c^{70}Q_c^{70} + P_b^{70}Q_b^{70} + P_o^{70}Q_o^{70}) = \text{CON}^{70}}$$

$$= \left(\frac{P_c^{71} - P_c^{70}}{P_c^{70}}\right)\frac{P_c^{70}Q_c^{70}}{\text{CON}^{70}} + \left(\frac{P_b^{71} - P_b^{70}}{P_b^{70}}\right)\frac{P_b^{70}Q_b^{70}}{\text{CON}^{70}} + \left(\frac{P_o^{71} - P_o^{70}}{P_o^{70}}\right)\frac{P_o^{70}Q_o^{70}}{\text{CON}^{70}}$$

(CON = consumption)

Note that the fraction in parentheses is the percentage change in each commodity price and that it is multiplied by the proportion or share of base-period expenditure on the good.

Obviously the change in the cost of living for the economy as a whole may be inappropriate for different individuals, because their spending patterns may be different from the average. In our example, notice that prices have risen 25 percent for the automobile buff who buys no bread or no oranges, while prices have remained constant for the vitamin C man who lives by oranges alone.

The U. S. Department of Labor periodically conducts consumer surveys to determine the appropriate weights to be used in constructing the official U. S. cost of living price index. The 1963 shares or weights of various commodity groups are shown in Table 2.2.

TABLE 2.2

Weights of Major Groups in Consumer Price Index[2]

Food	28.2%
Housing	30.7
Apparel and Upkeep	10.7
Transportation	11.7
Health	18.0
	100.0%

If your consumption patterns are different from those shown in the table, your individual cost of living has probably behaved differently from the inflation figures published in the newspapers.

What Price Indices Are

We have learned how to calculate changes in the cost of living, but we do not yet know how to get an aggregate price series itself. What would we learn if we made an average of the prices of cars, bread, and fruit? Would this average price be

[2] SOURCE: Bureau of Labor Statistics, "The Consumer Price Index, Technical Notes 1959–63," Bulletin No. 1554 (Washington, D.C., 1967).

interesting to us, even if we could construct it? Generally we are more interested in how prices change over time than we are in their absolute level. Thus economists traditionally ignore absolute prices and express prices as percentages of their value in some particular year. Expressing price as a percentage of its base year value converts a price *series* into a price *index*. To construct a price index, we arbitrarily choose a base year and divide the prices in all other years by the price in that base year. The price index shows at a glance the percentage changes in price since the base year. All goods are comparable, because all are expressed in terms of percentage deviations from a common base.

The construction of price indices is illustrated in Table 2.3.

TABLE 2.3

Sample Price Indices

Year	Price Series		Price Indices	
	Cars	Bread		
0	2,000	0.50	100	100
1	2,500	0.60	125	120
2	3,000	0.70	150	140
3	3,200	0.75	160	150

Formally the price index of good i in year j is $P_i^j = \dfrac{P_i^j}{P_i^o} \times 100$, the ratio of the price in year j to the price in the base year.

As one would guess from our previous discussion of aggregation, an aggregate price index is simply a weighted average of individual price indices where the weights are the shares of the individual commodities in the base period.

Difference between Nominal and Deflated Magnitudes

One of the main uses of price indices is to separate changes in economic magnitudes like GNP or aggregate consumption due to changes in prices from those due to changes in production or real purchasing power. For example, we read in the newspapers that GNP in 1969 was $932 billion compared to $504 billion in 1960. Some part of the large increase is only a change in prices, and we use a price index to find out exactly what part. We have already seen that a price index measures change due to price. If, therefore, we divide GNP in 1969 by the GNP price index for 1969, we have 1969 GNP in base period prices ($932 billion ÷ 128 = $728 billion); $728 billion is what GNP would have been in 1969 had there been no change in prices since 1958, the base year. We call this magnitude "real," or deflated, GNP, which we will write as GNP_R. Current, or nominal, GNP will be denoted GNP_N. The nominal value of any variable is its value in current money prices, while its real, or deflated, value is its value in terms of the prices of some base period.

Let us refer to our consumption example (Table 2.1). Nominal consumption rose by 26.5 percent in 1971. Setting 1970 as the base year, the 1971 price index is 115.[2] Thus, real consumption is $1,265,000/1.15 = $1,100,000. Comparing this with the base period, we see that real consumption has increased by 10 percent. Thus the 26.5 percent increase in nominal consumption resulted from a 15 percent increase in prices and a 10 percent increase in goods purchased (1.10 × 1.15 = 1.265).

We have said that a deflated, or real, variable is the same as current quantities valued at base period prices. Let us see if this is true for our example. We add 1971 quantities valued at 1970 prices.

	1970 Prices	×	1971 Quantity	=	Deflated, or "Real" Consumption
$C_R =$	$2,000	×	110	=	220,000
+	0.50	×	1,100,000	=	550,000
+	0.30	×	1,100,000	=	330,000
					$1,100,000

---

[2]
$$P_{71} = [0.2 \frac{2500}{2000} + 0.5 \frac{0.60}{0.50} + 0.3 (\frac{0.30}{30})] \times 100$$
$$= 0.2 (125) + 0.5 (120) + 0.3 (100)$$
$$= 115$$

14

The figure $1,100,000 is the amount that would have been spent on consumption in 1971 if prices had not changed. The example demonstrates that real, or deflated, magnitudes can be obtained either by dividing a current value by a price index or by adding quantities valued in base period prices.

Real values are useful, because they tell us about quantities. In 1970 nominal GNP increased by 4.8 percent. In fact Washington rejoiced over our becoming the first $1 trillion economy. But does this tell us that production had increased? No, it does not; for real GNP fell. All that growth was an illusion of rising prices, which one discovers by observing what happened to real GNP.

Costs of Inflation

We now know what inflation is, how it is calculated, how it is reported in the newspapers, and some of the jargon to be used in discussing it. We still do not know if inflation is bad or good, how it is caused, or what it does to an economy. Why is inflation disliked and feared? Is it bad for everyone or only for bankers? These questions concern us next.

No one can afford to be indifferent about the future rate of inflation in a monetary economy. Most contracts—mortgages, labor agreements, bank deposits—are specified in dollars. Inflation is a reduction in the purchasing power of a dollar. Inflation decreases the amount of goods the holder of a dollar may obtain in exchange for his dollar.

One bad thing about inflation is that its impact on different groups is decidedly unequal. A person on a fixed income or holding assets fixed in nominal terms loses; a person who can adjust the prices of items he has for sale is protected. The person who owes money (a debtor) is at an advantage, because the repayment of his debts requires less sacrifice of future goods. By the same token the creditor loses, because he is repaid with dollars that will buy fewer goods than when he lent dollars. People on pensions and holders of government bonds, life insurance policies, or bank deposits are creditors who obviously lose during an inflation. One can regard inflation as a kind of tax which reduces purchasing power, as all taxes

15

do. It is a very discriminatory tax, falling unequally on different groups of taxpayers in the economy.

Another cost of inflation is that it causes the economic system to operate inefficiently. Because inflation may involve income loss, it is reasonable to expect people to try to protect themselves against that possibility. In doing so they devote time and resources which could have been used in leisure or production. For example, people find it costly to hold currency and checking accounts because of the loss in purchasing power as prices rise. They try to get along with less than they would under stable prices by keeping smaller balances and by buying inflation-proof assets with the difference. The motive for holding money is the greater convenience it allows in making transactions. With smaller money holdings, people find they must make more trips to the bank to deposit and withdraw funds. Thus inflation causes a loss of convenience or leisure.

Business also takes steps to protect itself from inflation. It becomes worthwhile to use labor to collect bills more rapidly, because unpaid bills, like any other nominal debt, cause a loss in purchasing power. This same labor could be used to produce things, rather than to reduce inflation-caused financial losses. Thus inflation causes a misallocation of labor, both for the consumer and for business. In an inflation, investors find it profitable to speculate in inventory. The demand for houses, paintings, and Swiss bank accounts rises, because they are hedges against inflation. This too is unproductive, because the savings could have been used to finance real additions to the capital stock of the economy.

Because inflation can so profoundly affect the distribution of income and wealth in a monetary economy, will not individuals try to defend themselves from it? Of course they will. Let us see what kind of actions might be taken by different groups.

Inflation and Labor

Consider the problem for the worker. Most workers work under contracts that run for one year or longer. Salary levels

16

are agreed upon at the beginning of the contract. To the worker the salary represents the command over goods that he obtains in return for his work. He is interested in the number of dollars he earns, because dollars represent the right to buy a certain quantity of goods and services. Unless the worker derives pleasure out of owning dollar bills, he is concerned with the number of refrigerators or loaves of bread his day's work will earn. Clearly the number depends on price changes that occur over the life of his labor contract. He is paid a salary in dollars, and the purchasing power of those dollars changes if there is inflation. The worker cannot, therefore, think only in terms of his nominal wage. He must convert the dollars he earns into an equivalent number of refrigerators and loaves of bread. He does this by deflating or dividing his wage by an index that represents his cost of living. The real wage, W/P, represents his command over goods. If W/P falls, he is working for less in real terms, regardless of how much his nominal wage has risen.

As an illustration, suppose a certain group of workers are willing to work for a wage of $2 an hour. Suppose also that the price index is 100, so that W/P is 2.00. The workers, expecting no inflation, sign a one-year contract for an hourly wage of $2. During the course of the year, however, prices rise by 10 percent. By the end of the year, the workers discover that they are actually working for 2.00/1.10 = $1.80 an hour. That is, they can buy only as many goods with their $2 wage as they could have bought originally with a wage of $1.80 an hour. The following year the workers demand a return to the real wage of $2, which means a nominal wage of $2.20. Once again they are acting as if they expected no inflation, because if inflation continues at 10 percent, they will find that they were again working for a real wage of less than $2 for most of the year. Income is being redistributed from them to their employers by the inflation, *because* they did not anticipate it.

Alternatively, if this same group of workers realize that inflation will recur each year, they will attempt to push their real wage above $2 at the beginning of the year. In that way the real wage will be above its desired level for part of the year and below it for the rest. The two parts should offset each other, so that on average the real wage is at its desired level.

The point is that labor must make some forecast of inflation, and the larger that forecast becomes, the larger the wage increases demanded by labor will be.

Expected Inflation and Financial Markets

Laborers are not the only ones whose behavior is influenced by their forecast of inflation. Expected inflation also has an important impact on the way the public holds its wealth, and thereby on the terms of borrowing. Financial loans are contracts specifying repayment in future dollars. The lender transfers present purchasing power to the borrower, and he expects the same amount of purchasing power returned to him in the future plus some interest for its use. Like the laborer, he is not interested in the number of dollars being returned to him, but in the command over resources that the dollars represent. He too must make a forecast of inflation to be expected during the loan period. If prices are rising at 5 percent a year, the lender needs an interest rate of 5 percent just to recover the real value of the money he lends. Thus the interest rate he charges is likely to be equal to his forecast of inflation plus whatever interest rate he would have charged had he expected no inflation.

Therefore we must make a distinction between real and nominal interest rates, just as we did between real and nominal wages. The nominal interest rate will equal the real rate plus the expected rate of inflation. We should observe a rise in nominal interest rates during inflations, because lenders learn to expect inflation. This may explain a good deal of the variation in the nominal interest rates in the United States, as shown in Table 2.4. Despite all the talk about extraordinarily high interest rates during the past several years, when a correction for inflation is made, the residual rate, which we could call the real rate, is lower now than it was during the early 1960s.

Expected inflation induces the public to try to change the composition of its wealth. At any moment there exists a cer-

TABLE 2.4

Real and Nominal Interest Rates

Year	Corporate Bond Rate (Moody's Aaa) (1)	Rate of Inflation (GNP Deflator) (2)	Real Rate of Interest (1) — (2)
1950	2.62	1.5	1.12
1955	3.06	1.2	1.86
1956	3.36	3.3	1.06
1957	3.89	3.6	.29
1958	3.79	2.2	1.59
1959	4.38	1.6	2.78
1960	4.41	1.7	2.71
1961	4.35	1.3	3.05
1962	4.33	1.1	3.23
1963	4.26	1.3	3.16
1964	4.40	1.5	2.90
1965	4.40	1.9	2.50
1966	5.13	2.7	2.43
1967	5.51	3.2	2.31
1968	6.18	4.0	2.18
1969	7.03	4.7	2.33

tain stock of money, bonds, equities, houses, and other physical capital. Some of these assets protect the holder against inflation, others do not. When a change is expected in the amount of future inflation, the demand for inflation-proof assets should rise and the demand for other assets should fall. This should cause the price of inflation-proof assets to rise in relation to the others.

Consider outstanding bonds. Bonds are pieces of paper promising to pay the owner a certain number of dollars in interest each year plus a fixed amount of principal at some specified future time. Once again the holder, or buyer, of that security has the problem of distinguishing between the number of dollars he will receive and the real value of those dollars. Suppose a corporate bond was issued some time in the past when the rate of interest was 5 percent. That bond was sold

19

originally at $1000 and paid yearly interest of $50.[3] During the current year, however, expected inflation has risen by 2 percent, making the current nominal interest rate 7 percent. What happens to the price of our 5 percent bond? Clearly no buyer will pay $1000 to receive a $50 yearly income, because he can earn $70 with that same amount by buying a newly issued bond. Rather, he will pay an amount such that 7 percent of it equals $50 (bond price = $50/.07 = $714). The bond price falls to $714.

The rise in expected inflation costs our bondholder dearly. The market price of his bond falls by almost 30 percent. To put it another way, whenever the expected rate of inflation rises, all future contracts denominated in current dollars become less attractive as ways of holding wealth, because the store of purchasing power they represent falls. Bonds are a good example of such a contract. Therefore one can expect their price to fall in relation to other assets.

The characteristic that makes an asset a good hedge against inflation is its ability to maintain its value in relation to goods, that is, its purchasing power. Bonds do not do this, as we have seen, but durable goods do. As prices go up, relative prices of various physical goods generally remain fairly constant, so the rate of exchange between one good and another does not change. The man who invests his savings in houses, diamonds, or land finds that the amount of goods he had to give up to buy his assets is just about the same as the amount he gets back when he sells them, regardless of the inflation. Whenever the public's expected rate of inflation rises, therefore, the demand for physical assets should increase and the demand for financial assets should decrease. Because the amount of all these assets is fixed at any moment, an increase in expected inflation should increase the price of the physical assets in relation to the financial ones. A person will be willing to hold the financial assets only when their nominal return is so high that they yield the same real return as physical assets.

---

[3] Assume, for simplicity, that the redemption date is far enough in the future that we can ignore the effect of inflation on the repayment of the principal.

For bonds, as we have seen, this equilibrium can occur only after there are substantial losses for bondholders.

In countries with long histories of rapid inflation, or in hyperinflation, there is a flight from all financial assets into physical goods. It becomes impossible to sell bonds, and the public holds all its savings in the form of land, buildings, cars, or even inventories of canned goods. We have all heard the story of the Latin American saver holding his wealth in jewelry and houses, or of the German during the hyperinflation of the 1920s who took his pay at noon and rushed out to convert it into goods before nightfall to avoid the loss of purchasing power during the afternoon. This is not irrational behavior at all; it is instead a very sensible reaction to high rates of expected inflation.

Questions

1. Why would we not expect the relative prices of various physical assets to be affected by an inflation?
2. Periodically, the government changes the base year for its price indices. Why is this necessary? Can you think of any defects inherent in price indices?
3. We normally say that creditors tend to suffer real income losses during an inflation. Would this be true of all inflations or only of unanticipated ones?
4. Is it possible for creditors, labor groups, and others to protect themselves from real income losses during unanticipated inflations? during anticipated inflations?

Suggestions for Further Reading

Cagan, Philip, "The Monetary Dynamics of Hyperinflation," in Milton Friedman ed., *Studies in the Quantity Theory of Money.* Chicago: University of Chicago Press, 1956.

Kessel, R. A., and A. A. Alchian, "Effects of Inflation," *Journal of Political Economy* (December 1962), 521–537.

Stigler, George, *et al.*, *The Price Statistics of the Federal Government.* New York: National Bureau of Economic Research, 1961.

3
CHAPTER

Inflation
and the
Labor Market

The labor market is the principal factor in our analysis of the inflationary process, because the reaction by workers and business to price changes gives inflation it's powerful effect on output and employment. In this chapter we show the conditions determining employment and wages and how they are affected by inflation, both foreseen and unforeseen. We demonstrate that the higher the forecast of inflation by labor, the lower the level of employment. When we combine this with the likely ways of forecasting, we get a cyclic pattern of employment and price changes which agrees closely with actual United States experience.

Demand for Labor

Let us look first at the determination of wages in an imaginary world where all jobs and all workers are equivalent. This situation requires an analysis of supply and demand. Consider first the demand for labor by the firm.

How much labor is the firm willing to employ at different wage rates? Just like any other buyer, the employer **hires** labor services (man-hours) so long as their value to him is at least as great as their cost. From his knowledge of the production process, the businessman knows just how many extra widgets an additional worker can produce. Because he also knows the price of widgets, he can calculate the extra revenue he will receive from employing an additional man. The businessman can then compare the cost of that man to see if it is profitable to hire him. The employer is in business to earn maximum profit; he should therefore hire workers so long as the extra revenue they produce exceeds the wage they must be paid.

The additional revenue generated by each additional man is called marginal revenue product (MRP). It is equal to the marginal physical product of labor (MPP, the number of extra widgets) multiplied by the price of widgets. Then the profit-maximizing businessman follows this simple rule: Make the MRP of the last man hired just equal to his wage. The firm hires men until the extra revenue produced by one man just equals what he has to be paid.

$$\text{Maximum profit rule: Wage} = \text{MRP, last man} \quad (3.1)$$

If we know the wage rate, the price of widgets, and the schedule of extra widgets produced by extra labor, we should be able to predict how many men the firm will employ and how many widgets can be produced.

Suppose an individual widget maker produces under the conditions shown below.

Labor Man-Days	Total Output (Widgets/Day)	MPP (Number of Widgets Produced by Last Man)	Price	MRP
1	20	20	$10	$200
2	35	15	10	150
3	45	10	10	100
4	50	5	10	50
5	53	3	10	30
6	55	2	10	20
7	56.5	1.5	10	15

If the wage is $20 a day, the firm following the above rule will hire six men and will produce 55 widgets. That will maximize total profit-revenue minus labor costs.[1]

The product schedule of the widget firm has what we call diminishing returns or productivity. That is, the MPP per extra man decreases as more men are hired. Diminishing returns is an assumption, but a number of important results follow from it, so we should understand its rationale. In drawing up our product schedule, we are assuming that fixed capital and management resources are constant. When the firm hires extra labor, the amount of machinery and management per man falls. Output per man should depend positively on capital and management per man, so that the MPP of additional men declines. Diminishing returns follows from the fact that the supply of machines is constant at any moment of time. Over time, if the firm invests in new machines, the product schedule will rise, allowing the firm to increase employment.

In general, we would expect that the higher the wage, the fewer men employed; this is clearly true for the widget firm. For example, at a wage of $25 per man-day, the firm would hire only five men, the reason being diminishing returns. If the wage rises, the employer must contract his labor force until MPP increases by an equal amount. If employment is to be increased, either the wage must fall or prices must rise. To say the same thing in another way, the real wage, W/P, must fall.

In Chapter 2 we learned that the real wage is the nominal wage deflated by the price index. W/P is then the rate of exchange between labor and goods—the amount of goods the businessman has to give up to buy a man-day of labor. In our example the real wage is $20/$10 = 2$, or two widgets per man-day. With this in mind we can now reinterpret equation 3.1; it can be written as

$$W/P = MPP_{\text{last man}}$$

---

[1] In our example the firm is indifferent between hiring five and six men, because the numbers we have presented show the MPP as being equal to two widgets for all levels of employment between five and six.

In other words our maximum profit rule can be restated: Make the MPP of the last man hired just equal to the real wage. Furthermore, because MPP decreases as the labor force increases, we know that the firm will want to increase employment only if the real wage decreases.

We can summarize our discussion by stating that under the assumption of diminishing returns to labor, the relation between the quantity of labor demanded and the real wage will be negative. This relation is depicted graphically by the conventional demand curve *DD* shown in Figure 3.1. What *DD* says or represents is that the higher the real wage, the fewer laborers hired, and the lower the real wage, the higher the employment.

Our discussion of labor demand has been carried out at the firm level, but the shape of the labor demand curve for the entire economy should be the same. Each firm maximizes profits by hiring labor until the wage of the last worker just equals his MRP. If the demand curve for each firm has the same downward slope, this downward slope is preserved when we aggregate over all firms. We can interpret *DD* in Figure 3.1 as an economy-wide demand curve for labor which says that employment depends negatively on the real wage. The reason for this is that the capital stock available to the economy is fixed at any moment, as it is for the firm. There are only a certain number of machines available to the labor force, so that the additional product of new employment should be falling. Of course, fixed investment by the economy over time will push the labor demand curve to the right, just as it will for the firm.

Supply of Labor

Having discussed the aggregate demand curve for labor, we are left with the problem of the labor supply curve. Before discussing this problem, however, we should distinguish a number of different concepts of labor supply. The first is the number of hours of labor supplied, which will be different from the second concept, number of people working, whenever hours per day or days per month change. Finally, labor supply may mean the number of men *willing* to work instead of the

The Labor Market

Figure 3.1

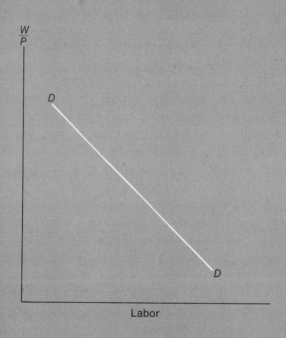

number *actually* working. The former, known as the *labor force*, differs from the latter by the number of unemployed. The unemployed are members of the labor force; that is, they are willing to work, but they are temporarily unemployed while they are searching for a better job.

We now return to the problem of determining the labor supply curve. If we are interested in the total labor force, we seek a relation indicating the number of people willing to work at various wage rates. If actual employment is our primary concern, the supply curve should show the number of people actually working at various wage rates.

Labor contracts are expressed in nominal wages, but we have already claimed that a worker is interested in the command over resources which he gains in exchange for giving up his leisure. Dollars are not useful in themselves but only for what they will buy. The worker should be thinking of the real, not the nominal, wage. The real wage tells exactly how many goods the worker will receive per day of leisure foregone. The labor supply curve, for whatever concept of supply we adopt, should therefore show the relation between supply and the real wage.

For convenience, assume that the number of hours of labor services each worker provides is fixed. We can then translate the business demand for a number of hours of *labor services* into a demand for a *number of workers*. Our labor market diagram will then be shown in terms of number of men employed instead of number of man-days. This simplifies the analysis and is also defensible in light of the institutional constraints on the ability to vary the length of the work week or work year in response to wage variations.

We are left with two labor supply curves to derive, the labor force and the number of employed. What does the labor force supply curve look like? It might seem natural to expect that a rise in real wages would bring more people into the labor force. After all, the rise in W/P increases the return to work. But most heads of families are not free to enter or leave the labor force in response to wage variations. They may accept unemployment as they look for a better job, but they do not leave the labor force. The source of any potential fluctuations in the size of the labor force must therefore be sought in the secondary labor force composed primarily of working wives.

A rise in real wages may well bring nonworking wives into the labor force. It is equally possible, however, that as the real wage of the head of the family rises, he uses part of that extra income to buy leisure for his wife. We have two opposite effects—on the one hand, the rise in real wages makes working more attractive for wives; on the other, it also increases family income and the demand for leisure.

In the absence of any firm conviction or knowledge about which effect dominates, we will assume that one offsets the other. We are thus asserting that a rise in the real wage neither increases nor decreases the number of people willing to work. In terms of Figure 3.2 we are saying that the labor force supply curve is vertical.[2]

This number of people willing to work that has been under discussion is the labor force, not the number employed. The difference between the two is, of course, unemployment. To understand what the supply of labor employed is, we must take a closer look at unemployment. What are its economic determinants and what is its economic purpose?

A man is unemployed when he is in the labor force but is devoting full time to seeking a better job. The cost of his unemployment is the wages he would have earned, and the benefit is the higher paying job he might find by his search. This type of unemployment stems from imperfections in the labor market. Jobs and workers are not perfectly alike and information is not perfect. Each worker has an idea of the real wage he should be able to command. But he does not know where such a job vacancy exists, and one alternative way of finding it is to devote full time to a job search. Unemployment is a way of gathering information about the job market in a world where information is costly.

One way of conceptualizing the unemployment decision

[2] For further literature and evidence on labor participation rates, see Glen G. Cain, "Unemployment and the Labor Force Participation of Secondary Workers," *Industrial and Labor Relations Review* (January 1967), 275–297, and Belton Fleisher, *Labor Economics: Theory and Evidence*, 73–91. Englewood Cliffs, N. J.: Prentice-Hall, 1970.

stems from Phelps.[3] Imagine the economy as a set of separate islands with one factory on each. Information about local island wage rates is perfect, but can be obtained for other islands only by visiting each island and sampling its labor market. In other words, to be certain of the opportunities elsewhere, a laborer must leave work and travel around the neighboring islands. When is it rational for him to become unemployed? Whenever he thinks that the future increase in wages he will get by moving more than compensate him for the days of current wages lost through unemployment. In the rarefied world of perfect information and foresight, unemployment would not occur. Each worker on each island would know exactly what his opportunities were. Because all wage rates for equivalent work would be equal (why?), search and unemployment would be irrational. Why, for example, would a carpenter ever quit his job for a better paying one if there were one economy-wide wage rate for carpenters? Unemployment is rational only where jobs are not all alike and information is not perfect. Unemployment occurs when a man believes he can increase his lifetime earnings by devoting full time to searching for a better paying job. We could call this sort of unemployment *frictional* unemployment, and we should note that such unemployment is beneficial to labor, because it is a way of increasing earnings in a world of imperfect and costly information. We should also note that frictional unemployment is not a result of low wages per se, but a result of wages being lower than those a man expects to find by looking further.

The frictionally unemployed are a revolving pool of people acquiring information about their opportunities by devoting full time to a search of the job market. They have certain expectations about the level of real wages they desire and should be able to command. The expectations are based on what other people in the same profession are earning, hearsay, newspaper advertisements, and other factors. These unemployed will be traveling from job opening to job opening, looking for the job that meets their expectations. Presumably, as their period of

[3] E. S. Phelps, "Money Wage Dynamics and Labor Market Equilibrium," *Journal of Political Economy* (July–August 1968).

unemployment becomes longer, they scale down those expectations until they finally find an acceptable job.

At any point in time, what would it take to reduce the level of frictional unemployment? Remember that each unemployed worker is searching for an acceptable real wage. If there should be a general rise in real wages, some of the unemployed would find jobs and wages meeting or exceeding their expectations. In other words, a rise in the average real wage should reduce the level of frictional unemployment. Conversely, we could say that a rise in the real wage increases the number of people actually working.

We can now summarize all this discussion by completing the labor market diagram. In Figure 3.1 we showed the demand for labor. Now we add two new curves (see Figure 3.2). LL shows the total labor force. Because, by our assumptions, it is fixed at any point, and is not affected by the real wage, it is a vertical line. (The line will be shifting to the right over time, as the labor force expands along with the population.) SS could be called a "willingness to accept employment" schedule. It shows the number of people who actually have jobs as a function of the real wage. The distance between SS and LL is unemployment. SS is upward sloping, because of our assertion that as real wages rise, more and more of the unemployed find wage offers in line with their expectations and accept jobs.

Determination of Equilibrium Employment and Wages

Equilibrium in any market is defined as a state in which the quantity supplied equals the quantity demanded or where the market clears. In the labor market, equilibrium will occur at that real wage rate at which employers are willing to hire all the men willing to work. Geometrically, we are looking for a point on both the supply and the demand curves. In Figure 3.2, this is obviously point A, the intersection of the two curves. At that equilibrium, employment is L_e, unemployment is the distance L_f-L_e, and the real wage is W/P_e.

If the real wage was lower, there would be an excess demand for labor. Some jobs would be unfilled, because the jobholders would have left work to seek higher wages else-

Supply and Demand in the Labor Market

Figure 3.2

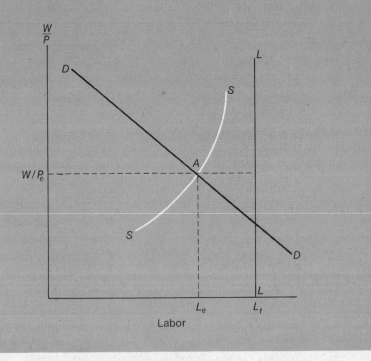

where. As business tries to fill the vacancies, it is forced to raise its wage offers. The process continues until the real wage rises to its equilibrium level, W/P_e.

This world we have sketched is quite hazy on how the prices of goods are determined and how they are perceived by employers and workers. Yet these perceptions are crucial, because both employers and employees think in terms of the real wage rate, not the nominal. In Chapter 4 the goods market and the determination of the aggregate price level will be analyzed in detail. Here we note that the equilibrium in the goods market and that in the labor market are determined in such a way that the level of wages influences the equilibrium price level and vice versa.

In our labor market we have implicitly assumed that everyone knows the equilibrium price level and can therefore immediately convert any nominal wage into a real wage. If he has perfect foresight about present and future rates of inflation, no one will regret his decision. What if the forecasts are wrong?

In the real world, labor contracts often cover a long period. They require forecasts of price changes for more than one market period. Auto workers sign two-year contracts; steel and aluminum workers sign three-year contracts. Even one-year contracts require price forecasts. We argue that the forecasting problem is more difficult for labor than it is for the firm, because the relevant price to the firm is the price of his product, one single price in a market it knows well. Labor, however, has to worry about the entire cost of living. Remember that the worker is interested in the general purchasing power of his wage, and he calculates this by deflating his money wage by a general cost of living index. He has to forecast the prices of housing, medical services, food, and all the other products he uses. Management has to forecast only one price. In our world, laborers accept job offers contingent upon what they *think* the real wage is and will be. Yet they probably have a very dim perception of the path of future prices throughout the economy. It is therefore entirely possible that when the future arrives, there will be a difference between the real wage they once thought they would earn and the one they actually earn. In the real world, there is no reason to assume that labor and management base their plans on the same set of price forecasts. There could thus be a difference between the labor supply and demand curves as perceived by management and by labor. What occurs to our labor market when these elements of realism are introduced?

Effect of Unexpected Inflation on Employment

We are going to trace the adjustment to unexpected inflation by the labor market. To do this we will need to follow the market over a number of market periods, a market period being a length of time during which the supply and demand curves do not change. With unexpected inflation we must distinguish between what we could call the labor supply curve as perceived by labor and the actual curve as observed by management.

The perceived labor supply curve shows the number of men holding jobs as a function of what they think the real wage is. The actual supply curve shows the actual real wage at which that number of men is working. The difference between the two curves results from the difference between expected and actual prices. To find an equilibrium real wage and an employment level for any period, we simply find the intersection of that period's actual labor demand and supply curves.

To start the process, imagine an economy in equilibrium with constant prices which is disturbed by an unexpected rise in government spending. As we shall see, this will cause a rise in prices throughout the economy. Following our assumption about labor's imperfect forecast of the general price level, suppose that this inflation is entirely unexpected by labor, which forecasts a continuation of the price level of the previous period. Each unemployed worker is searching for an acceptable wage offer. In his mind he is deflating that wage offer by a forecast price level. If he expects no inflation, the prices he uses are last year's price level. If, however, unknown to him, prices are rising this year (that is, unexpected inflation), there will be a difference between the perceived real wage and the actual real wage represented by any nominal wage. Labor acts on the basis of what it perceives the real wage to be.

Thus we amend our diagram of the labor market to include

a perceived labor supply curve, S_pS_p, and an actual labor supply, S_aS_a (Figure 3.3). Whenever prices rise unexpectedly, S_aS_a lies to the right of S_pS_p. L_0 men continue to offer to work at the old nominal wage level even though the rise in prices has reduced the purchasing power that wage represents. It is as if, suddenly, labor is willing to work for lower real wages.

Suppose that previously the labor market equilibrium was at L_0. Now, owing to the shift in the actual labor supply curve, employment rises to L_1. Why does that occur? The inflation fools some workers. Take the extra workers between L_0 and L_1. That many people leave unemployment and go to work, because they receive the increase in nominal wages they were looking for; but they do not realize that this increase is being more than offset by rising prices. Management finds that actual real wages are lower and is able to hire more men, while the men think, incorrectly as it turns out, that real wages have risen. Unexpected inflation thus appears to be a costless way of increasing employment.

We can imagine how the rise in prices causes the increase in employment or the decrease in unemployment. The frictionally unemployed have certain nominal wages at which they are willing to work. If prices are rising, employers can afford to raise the nominal wages they pay and the unemployed workers are likely to find an acceptable wage offer and take a job. The rise in prices has reduced frictional unemployment.

Observe carefully what is taking place. The government-spending program causes a rise in prices, increased employment, and a fall in real wages. Consider how this process works at the individual factory. Take our widget firm, for example. At the price of $10 and a wage rate of $20, we saw that the factory employed six men. Suppose that the price of widgets rises to $13.33 and the wage remains at $20. The MRP of any worker will then have risen, producing the revised MRP schedule shown below.

Labor	MRP
4	$66.50
5	40.00
6	26.67
7	20.00

Labor Market When Expected Inflation Is Different from Actual Inflation

Figure 3.3

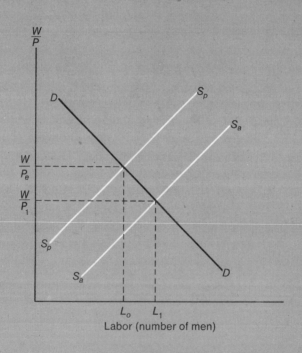

By our rule of equating the wage to the MRP of the last worker, it is now profitable to employ the seventh worker. The rise in prices allows an increase in employment.

Employment increases because of the apparent willingness of workers to work for lower real wages in period 1. Are they willing because labor has suddenly become more tractable and less aggressive in wage negotiations? Obviously not. The inflation has caught them by surprise. They still think that prices are at period 1 levels, so that when management offers higher wages, job acceptances by the unemployed rise, even though prices also are rising. The first-period inflation therefore increases employment and with it output, but only because the inflation was unexpected by workers. Had they perceived it, those extra workers between L_o and L_1 would have realized that the rise in nominal wages and prices did not represent the increase in real wages they were looking for, and they would not have been willing to work.

Whenever there is a difference between what people expect and what actually occurs, there has to be an adjustment to the new reality. Labor is not likely to let this perception error in period 1 go uncorrected. The economy will discover that the increase in employment and output was temporary and not free.

Let us look at the labor market in market period 2. Labor has finally realized that prices did rise during period 1, and it is going to demand the appropriate increase in nominal wages to compensate for the price increases. People who were willing to work during period 1 for a certain wage rate no longer will be. Unless wages increase, there will be an increase in unemployment. How far do wages have to rise to equate supply and demand? Referring to Figure 3.3, S_pS_p was the supply curve of labor under the conditions shown. It still is; that is, if prices rose 10 percent in period 1, then in order to get L_o workers, nominal wages will have to rise by 10 percent. To get L_1 workers, wages must rise by more than 10 percent, on the assumption, of course, that labor expects no further inflation. The important thing about this process is that labor comes back to the supply curve S_pS_p. Unexpected inflation causes temporary departures, but they are reversed because they are not acceptable to labor. One could therefore call S_pS_p the long-run labor supply curve.

To make this discussion more concrete we can introduce a series of hypothetical wage, price, and employment data to represent the adjustment process and also put them on our labor market diagram. These data are shown in Table 3.2.

TABLE 3.2
Hypothetical Wage, Price, and Employment
in an Economy with Zero Expected Inflation

Period	Nominal Wage/Day	Price Index	Real Wage	Employment
Base	$10.00	100	$10.00	1,000,000
1	11.00	115	9.57	1,200,000
2	11.50	115	10.00	1,000,000

Nominal wages rise by $1 in period 1; this increase is interpreted by labor as an equivalent increase in real wages. The 15 percent rise in prices, however, more than offsets the increase, so that real wages fall to $9.57 and employment increases to 1.2 million. Suppose that labor continues to expect no further inflation during period 2. So that employment can continue to hold at 1.2 million, the *real* wage must rise to $11. This requires the nominal wage to rise to $12.65 (X/1.15 = $11.00). As we can see from Figure 3.4, businessmen do not find it profitable to pay so high a real wage to so many workers. If there is no further inflation, the labor market clears at a wage of $11.50 per day, the real wage at which the supply and demand curves intersect (11.50/1.15 = $10). Employment falls back to its long-run level of 1 million, because no further inflation is expected. The solution continues to hold until the conditions underlying the supply and demand curves change. The period 1 inflation causes a one-time upward jog in employment and output, after which the economy returns to its normal equilibrium levels. If labor really does think in terms of real wages, changing prices or nominal wages should at most have a short-run, temporary effect. The only way to increase employment permanently is either to increase the productivity of the labor force by investment in new machines or to persuade labor to work for lower real wages.

38

Labor Market in Hypothetical Economy with Unexpected Inflation

Figure 3.4

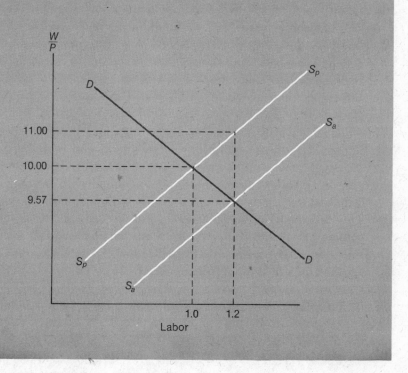

Effect of Expected Inflation on the Labor Market

Our initial description assumed that labor expected zero inflation throughout. When we drop that assumption, things change quite drastically. Suppose that instead of expecting no inflation at the start of period 2, the workers in our hypothetical economy expect the 15 percent inflation experienced during period 1 to continue. That is, they expect the price level during period 2 to rise from 115 to 132.225. Now merely making up for period 1 inflation will not protect the worker against further loss in purchasing power. Suppose he asks for a nominal wage of $11.50, enough to reestablish the desired real wage of $10 if there were no further inflation. Then at the projected 15 percent rise in prices, that $10 will be an effective real wage of 11.50/1.3225 = $8.70.

We can easily figure out what the potential labor supply will be at various nominal wages. Take the perceived supply curve S_pS_p of Figure 3.4 and convert nominal wages to real wages by using the expected price of 132.25, and then find the quantity of labor corresponding to that real wage in the perceived supply curve S_pS_p. One million men will work for $13.22 and 1.2 million will work for $12.60. A shift to positive expected inflation reduces the number of men willing to work at each nominal wage. Labor now demands an increase in wages to offset both the previous inflation and the expected future inflation.

So far we have dealt solely with expected prices. But we cannot determine equilibrium employment and real wages unless we know what happens to actual prices. Suppose that the rate of inflation during period 3 is actually 15 percent, the expected rate. Business will then be willing to hire 1.2 million men at a nominal wage of $W/1.3225 = 9.50$, or $12.56, and 1 million at $13.225. Thus we will find that the wage of $13.225, equal to a real wage of $10, will clear the labor market. The period 2 line of Table 3.2 becomes

Equilibrium When Expected Inflation Equals Actual Inflation

Period	Nominal Wage	Period Index	Real Wage	Employment
2	$13.225	1.3225	$10.00	1,000,000

In effect, when the price forecasts of labor are accurate, there is no difference between the perceived supply curve and the actual supply curve; the perceived curve is the actual curve. No adjustment for errors in forecasting is necessary, and the labor market is in equilibrium.

It is entirely possible for labor to overestimate future inflation. What occurs if the actual inflation is *less than* the 15 percent expected by labor? The nominal wage of $13.22, for example, will represent a real wage higher than $10 and can no longer be a market clearing wage level. Employment must fall below 1 million men. What occurs is that there is a difference between labor's perceived and actual supply curves just as there was for the unexpected inflation case, only this time the actual supply curve lies to the left of the perceived one. When labor expects more inflation than actually exists, in effect it demands higher real wages than it realizes. We can represent this on our diagram (Figure 3.5) as a new actual supply curve, $S_a^1 S_a^1$. Employment falls to 900,000 at a real wage of $11. The period 2 line of the table now becomes

Expected Inflation Greater Than Actual Inflation

Period	Nominal Wage	Price Index	Real Wage	Employment
2	132	120	11.00	900,000

This case is exactly parallel to the previous one, with reversed signs. With actual inflation greater than expected inflation, the actual labor supply curve lies to the right of the perceived curve. Employment rises temporarily above its equilibrium level at the intersection of $S_p S_p$ and *DD*. With expected inflation greater than actual inflation, the actual labor supply curve is $S_a^1 S_a^1$ to the left of $S_p S_p$. Employment temporarily falls below its equilibrium level and real wages rise.

Formation of Expectations

While the expected price level or the rate of inflation is apparently an important variable in the functioning of the

41

Labor Market When Actual Inflation Is Less Than Expected Inflation

Figure 3.5

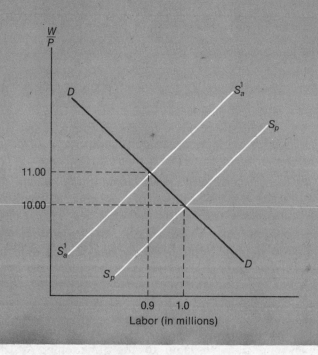

42

economy, the formation of expectations is something we do not know too much about. Forecasting is difficult and expensive, and it is probably efficient to use historical information or to project past experience. Expected inflation is probably a weighted average of actual past rates of inflation with some correction for significant current influences, such as the likelihood of war, crop failures, the availability of foreign exchange, or the government's determination to fight inflation. In general it is probably true that actual rates of inflation of the recent past play a most important part in forming expectations.

Whenever historical experience is a major determinant of expectations, an economy will be slow to adjust to changes in reality and the short-run adjustments by the system will be in quantities such as employment and output, as well as in prices. In Chapter 4 we will find that the long-run adjustment to a disturbance such as increased government spending will be a rise in prices with no change in output. With an expectations lag, however, prices are slow to move to their new levels. In the short run, part of the reaction by the economy is an increase in employment and output.

To anticipate our story somewhat, the slow adjustment of expectations to changes in the rate of inflation explains very well the typical cyclic pattern observed in an economy. At the beginning of the cycle, prices are stable and the first round of inflation comes as a surprise. We have called this first round the expansion phase of the inflationary process. Expected inflation is less than actual inflation, a situation that results in a rise in employment. At some point the government steps in to control the inflation; but by this time the public expects the inflation to continue. If the government actions are successful, they reduce the actual rate of inflation, probably below what people expected it to be. But when actual inflation is less than expected inflation, employment falls below its long-run equilibrium level. During what we have called the stabilization phase of an inflation, therefore, we should expect low levels of employment, while high levels should accompany the expansion phase. Both deviations stem from a difference between what labor expects prices to be and what they actually are. The cyclic pattern of employment results from imperfect foresight; it can be explained by the expectations lag.

Questions

1. What is the difference between the actual supply curve and the perceived supply curve of labor? When do the two curves diverge?
2. Assume that the marginal physical product of the last worker hired by a firm is 10 units per day and that the wage is $20 per day. With this information can you conclude anything about whether labor is expensive or cheap or whether the firm should hire or fire workers?
3. Under what conditions would we expect to find an increase in the money wage associated with a decrease in the quantity of labor demanded? with an increase in the quantity of labor demanded? with no change?
4. a) Is it ever rational for a person to enter the ranks of the unemployed voluntarily? Under what circumstances would he do this?
    b) Could we expect a rational, but unemployed, person to turn down job offers? Why?
    c) How might the decision to accept or to leave a job be affected by either anticipated or unanticipated inflation?
5. Why is the ratio of labor cost/dollars of sales a good measure of the real cost of labor? What is the difference between this measure and units of labor/unit of output?

Suggestions for Further Reading

Barbash, Jack, *American Unions: Structure, Government and Politics.* New York: Random House, 1967.

Bowen, William G., *Wage Behavior in the Postwar Period.* Princeton, N. J.: Princeton University Press, 1960.

Dunlop, John T., ed., *The Theory of Wage Determination.* London: St. Martin's Press, 1957.

Gordon, R. A., *The Goal of Full Employment.* New York: John
Wiley, 1967.

Kessel, R. A., and A. A. Alchian, "The Inflation-Induced Lag of
Wages," *American Economic Review* (March 1960), 43–66.

Reynolds, Lloyd G., "Wage Push and All That," *American Economic Review, Proceedings* (May 1960), 195–204.

4

CHAPTER

Inflation
and the
Goods Market

In Chapter 3 we studied the process by which employment and wages are determined. In this chapter we carry the analysis to the goods market, meaning the market for producible output. Here we show how the price and the quantity of output are determined in an economy. Equilibrium employment and real wages are found in the labor market by studying the intersection of the labor supply curve and the demand curve. We can use the same procedure in the goods market. We derive goods supply and demand curves, and their intersection determines aggregate output and the price level.

Supply and Demand for Individual Commodities

Let us examine the supply and the demand curves for individual commodities. Consider the beef market. The higher the price of beef, the more the ranchers are likely to produce. Because labor, hay, and fencing costs are still unchanged, it is going to be profitable to raise more cows or to feed each cow more so that it raises a heavier calf. On the demand side, as the price of beef rises, consumers switch to other kinds of meat; as the price falls, they buy more beef. Notice that we are making a key assumption; namely, that only the price of beef changes, while all other prices are constant. Under that assumption the supply curve in the individual market should be upward sloping, the demand curve downward sloping. The higher the price, the more the producers are willing to supply and the less the buyers are willing to buy.

Aggregate Demand and Supply

To simplify the analysis, assume that only one commodity is produced by the economy. The output of this good is equal to GNP, and changes in its price are the aggregate rate of inflation. What do the aggregate supply and demand curves look like?

Going from the analysis for an individual good to that for the aggregate is not as simple as may appear. Consider demand first. What occurs to aggregate demand when all prices change? Suppose prices for all goods rise by 10 percent. You may think the answer is obvious: of course demand will fall. But why will it fall? Suppose that the output of each good stays the same, even though prices rise; aggregate income will then rise by 10 percent. With nominal income 10 percent higher, why will people not be willing to pay 10 percent more for the same quantity of goods?

Consider our argument for the individual market. Demand falls for beef as prices rise, precisely because all other prices stay the same. If chicken, pork, fish, bread, and all other prices rise at exactly the same rate and if the consumer's income rises as well, it is difficult to argue that the consumer will buy less beef or any other product. In short, if everything rises at exactly the same rate as prices, there is no reason to suppose that rising aggregate prices decrease aggregate demand.

A change in prices that has no effect on any real, deflated variable should have no effect on demand. Such a change is similar to a government decree making ten old dollars equal to one new dollar—simply a change in units of accounts. But the rise in prices in an economy *does* have real effects. It is not the same as a change in units of account. It is like a govern-

47

ment decree stating that henceforth $1 will buy what 90 cents used to buy. The reason the two changes are different is because a rise in prices affects the distribution of income and the real value of savings, both of which affect aggregate demand.

Consider people who hold this savings in the form of currency and government bonds. These assets represent a certain command over resources which we find by deflating the nominal value by the price index. As prices rise, the real value of currency and government bonds falls. Holders of government debt are hurt by the rise in prices. There is a wealth effect. These people now have to save more to compensate for their loss of purchasing power, and their consumption demand should fall as prices rise. Because consumption is part of the aggregate demand for goods, this wealth effect is one reason that rising prices reduce aggregate demand.[1]

A rise in prices should raise the rate of interest and should reduce investment. Briefly, the interest rate is determined by the tastes of wealth holders and the portfolio of assets available to be held. A rise in prices changes that composition, because certain assets rise in price while others do not. Houses, machines, and other real goods rise in price; financial assets, such as bonds, bank deposits, and currency, do not. A rise in prices thus reduces the real purchasing power represented by financial assets, particularly money. Economists have presented quite convincing evidence that the rate of interest varies inversely with the real supply of money. Because rising prices reduce the real supply of money, interest rates should rise.

Continuing this interest rate effect, economic theory states that rising interest rates reduce the demand for capital and lower fixed investment in the short run. The financial effect of rising prices is a rise in interest rates and a drop in investment. Note that all this assumes that present inflation does not change expectations about future price changes. If

---

[1] It could be argued that we should not include government bonds in the wealth effect, because the real value of the future tax liability for repayment of the bonds falls with rising prices. The reduction in future taxes could just offset the loss of purchasing power on the bonds.

it did, we would have to distinguish between the nominal interest rate and the real interest rate. A rise in prices can reduce investment only if it raises the real interest rate.

Another reason that inflation reduces aggregate demand is that it changes the distribution of income, both within the private sector and between the private sector and the government. Both may affect the demand for consumption goods. Consider first the inflationary redistribution within the private sector. It is generally believed that inflation helps profits and hurts wages. The evidence from the United States economy suggests that inflation at the beginning of expansionary cycles does indeed shift the distribution of income away from labor. If profit earners have less propensity to consume than labor, transferring income from the latter to the former will reduce aggregate consumption. The same argument can be used for other transfers. Debtors generally gain during an inflation; creditors lose—because debts are specified in dollars. Rising prices change the real purchasing power represented by those dollars. To the extent that debtors have lower spending propensities than creditors, this transfer will again reduce aggregate consumption.

To our minds a more significant transfer is from the private sector to the government through progressive taxes. Income taxes are specified in dollars, and the rates are progressive. Furthermore the exemptions are expressed in nominal terms. As prices go up, the exemptions become lower and lower in real terms. An increase in nominal income exactly offset by an increase in prices pushes taxpayers into higher tax brackets with higher tax rates. A greater proportion of this income must be paid to the government as prices rise. Using actual United States tax rates, an individual with a taxable income of $20,000 pays a tax of $4380. Now suppose that prices and nominal income both rise by 10 percent. This individual's nominal taxable income is now $22,000 and his tax is $4380 plus 0.32 ($22,000 − $20,000) = $5020. In real terms (at prices of the initial year) taxes rise from $4380 to 5020/1.10 = $4560. In other words the tax receipts of the government rise by more than the cost of living, because the tax system is progressive.

The effect of inflation on government receipts is shown in Table 4.1. One has to be careful in comparing various years to be sure that there were no major changes in the tax system. The 1964–1967 period is one during which inflation accelerated and the tax system was more or less constant. True to our expectations, government receipts as a fraction of GNP rose continuously.

Personal consumption is related to disposable income. When an inflation redistributes purchasing power away from the private sector to the government, one would expect aggregate demand to fall.

To recapitulate, we have found three reasons why rising prices reduce demand. The first reason could be called a wealth effect; the second, an interest rate effect; the third, a redistribution effect. All three occur because price changes have real effects on the distribution of assets and income in the economy, a factor that changes aggregate behavior. There is nothing diabolical or bad in such a situation. A rise in prices should reduce demand.

TABLE 4.1

Effect of Inflation on Government Receipts

Year	Government Tax and Nontax Receipts / GNP	Inflation (GNP Deflator)
1961	27.8%	1.3%
1962	28.0	1.1
1963	28.6	1.3
1964 (tax cut)	27.5	1.5
1965	27.6	1.9
1966	28.4	2.7
1967	28.8	3.2
(1968 is not comparable because of the surtax)		

Effect of Inflation on Aggregate Supply

Consider now the shape of the aggregate supply curve. What would occur to output if prices of all goods changed? In

Chapter 3 we saw how a firm was able to increase employment and output when its selling price rose. We reproduce the relevant part of the production table for this firm as it illustrates the process by which price changes affect output in the goods market.

Labor	Total Units of Output	MPP	MRP at $P = \$10$	MRP at $P = \$13.33$
5	53.0	3.0	$30.00	$40.00
6	55.0	2.0	20.00	26.67
7	56.5	1.5	15.00	20.00

With a wage rate of $20 per day and a widget price of $10, the firm hires six men and produces 55 widgets. When prices rise by 33.3 percent it becomes profitable to increase production to 56½ widgets, because the rise in prices offsets the decline in MPP of the seventh worker. This conclusion should be fairly general. For any firm where the marginal output of additional workers drops, an increase in selling prices enables it to increase output. But notice a crucial assumption: the wage rate is constant. In other words we are showing what occurs to output if prices of all goods change while wages remain constant.

If the price of labor rises just as fast as prices, there can be no increase in output. Consider our widget maker. At a wage of $20 and a selling price of $13.33, he increases his output to 56½ widgets. But what if his workers demand 33⅓ percent increase in wages to compensate for the increase in prices? The new nominal wage rate will be $26.67, but the profit-maximizing output is still 55 widgets. In other words, when nominal wages are allowed to change along with the prices so that real wages are constant, price changes no longer allow firms to change their output.

Is it reasonable to suppose that wages would change with prices? Yes, indeed it is. Labor, we have argued, is interested in the real purchasing power represented by any nominal wage. Labor supply is drawn in terms of the real wage, not the nominal wage. One should expect, therefore, that any change in prices of goods will cause an equivalent change in nominal wages. Under these conditions inflation will have no effect on output. Only where wages do not change with prices will inflation have any effect on supply.

In one circumstance a change in prices does not lead to a change in nominal wages—this is when the change is not perceived by labor; that is, when it is unexpected. In Chapter 3 we explored in detail why labor might not clearly perceive price change in the short run and what would result when it did not. We showed how unexpected inflation allows firms to raise their nominal wage offers and how this leads to an increase in employment, because the unemployed think that the rise in nominal wages is also a rise in real wages. What is relevant to the goods market is that when employment rises, so does output. When a rise in prices is unexpected, therefore, both employment and output will increase. Conversely, if prices drop unexpectedly, employment and output drop.

We have shown that there is a positive relation between output and prices when price changes are not fully perceived or expected by labor. Because this perception error by the labor force is likely to be a short-run phenomenon, we should consider the positive association between prices and output as a *short-run* relation. In the long run, one must expect the labor force to demand a wage adjustment for every change in prices, because labor thinks in terms of the real wage. Thus, in the long run, price changes should have no effect on aggregate supply.

As in the labor market, we can summarize our discussion in the form of a picture of the relation between output and prices along the aggregate demand and supply curves (see Figure 4.1). We have already shown why aggregate demand falls with rising prices, that is, why the demand curve has a negative slope. The supply curve is more complicated; there are really two supply curves, one for fully perceived price changes and one for price changes unexpected by labor. We could call the latter the short-run aggregate supply curve, because it assumes that labor is taken by surprise by price changes, an assumption that is reasonable only in the short run. It is drawn upward sloping to show that as prices go up, employers can hire more labor and produce more output,

Aggregate
Goods Market

Figure 4.1

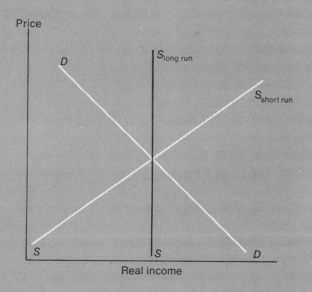

because nominal wages do not fully adjust. The long-run curve by contrast is vertical—in the long run, price changes do not change the real terms on which labor can be employed. When all prices including wages change equivalently, inflation does not increase the supply of goods, just what the vertical supply curve says.

Goods Market Equilibrium

As in the labor market, equilibrium is defined as a point at which buyers are willing to buy exactly what producers are willing to produce. Since the supply and demand curves are the collection of all the output-price combinations satisfactory to buyers and sellers, the equilibrium we are looking for is the intersection of the two curves, a point at which supply equals demand. Because we have two supply curves, we can speak of a short-run equilibrium using the short-run supply curve, and a long-run equilibrium using the long-run curve.

To understand how price and output are determined over time, we have only to analyze how the demand and supply curves shift. For example, if we find that the aggregate short-run supply curve shifts up over time while the demand curve is fixed, we predict a period of rising prices and falling output. If the demand curve shifts up while the supply curve is fixed, we expect rising prices and output.

Is There a Trade-off between Inflation and Output?

One question we have raised is whether there is a trade-off between inflation and output. Do rising prices bring more output? Our analysis of the goods market suggests an answer. From Figure 4.2 we can see that if the demand curve shifts to the right from D_1 to D_2 while the supply curves stay fixed, the short-run equilibrium will have higher prices and more output. Output rises from Q_1 to Q_2, prices rise from P_1 to P_2. If we are thinking of the long-run equilibrium, there will be only higher prices. Output remains at Q_1, while prices rise to P_3. Technically our analysis says that the trade-off between infla-

Goods
Market

Figure 4.2

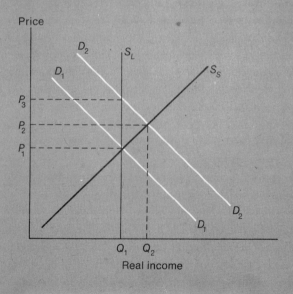

tion and output is a short-run phenomenon only. In the long run, prices have no effect on total production.

So much for the diagrams. Why are we getting this result? What is its meaning? The short-run supply curve is upward sloping instead of vertical, because of the assumption that nominal wages do not fully adjust to rising prices in the short run. If labor does not perceive short-run inflation, rising prices enable employers to hire more labor and to produce more output. Inflation enables the economy to pay higher nominal wages and to offset them with higher prices and more output. This is a short-run result, however, because it depends on the assumption of labor's erroneous price forecast. In a sense it can be said that unexpected inflation produces involuntary *overemployment.* Unemployed workers deflate their high wage offers by an erroneous price index and go to work; when employment rises, so of course does output. Thus if the reader accepts our assumption that labor makes erroneous price forecasts, or equivalently is slow to adjust nominal wages, then he must accept the implication that unexpected inflation results in a short-run increase in output and employment.

It is more important for the reader to understand why, in our view, there is no output effect of rising prices in the long run. Remember that in the long run we drop our assumption of imperfect foresight and deal with real wages. Every price change is met with an equal percentage change in nominal wage demands by those already working. Because employment is based on a comparison of labor's real product and the real wage, price changes have no employment effect. In the long run there is neither involuntary unemployment nor overemployment, so that the level of output the economy can produce is fixed by the technical conditions of labor's productivity and willingness to work.

This analysis leads to the far-reaching conclusion that the boom periods in our economic history, when both output and prices were rapidly rising, were probably years when inflation was higher than expected. Observe the record. Historically the early years of a boom such as that of 1965–1967 produce rising output and prices. In our interpretation, this output growth comes from the *change* in the rate of inflation, not from the *rate* of inflation itself. It is the change, and its unexpectedness, that produces the real results—because it puts the economy on a short-run supply curve. Of course such short-run boom results are not permanent. Every expansion is followed by its long-run supply curve. We will analyze the stabilization process in the following chapter.

Cost-Push and Demand-Pull Inflation

If observed prices are produced by the intersection of supply and demand curves, there can be only two reasons for rising prices, either rising demand or falling supply. When we speak of rising demand, we mean that more goods are demanded at each price, that the whole demand curve shifts to the right. Similarly with falling supply, we mean a leftward shift in the whole curve. Suppose that in the preceding market period the equilibrium price level was 100 and that consumers, investors, and the government together bought $900 billion worth of commodities. This year the government enters into a massive new spending program for which it does not tax the public. Because no spending power has been taken away from the public through taxes, there are now more buyers; at the old price level there is now excess demand. Prices rise to some new equilibrium point. You could think of the inflation as a kind of tax. Inflation acts as a tax on currency holders, and if the tax system is progressive, it reduces disposable income in the private sector. Rising prices allow the government to acquire the additional goods, because they reduce the spending of the private sector.

This kind of change in market conditions and the accompanying inflation used to be called demand-pull inflation. An economy started in equilibrium; demand then shifted to the right perhaps because war was declared, or because there was a massive increase in the money supply, or because new investment opportunities were discovered. The cause of the inflation was a shift in demand.

What used to be called cost-push inflation comes from a leftward shift in the supply curve. The most obvious cause of such a shift is a demand for higher nominal wages by labor. We know that a rise in wages will force each employer to cut

57

back output unless he can sell at higher prices. Taking all employers as a group, we find that the aggregate supply curve of the economy shifts to the left, from SS to S^1S^1 in Figure 4.3. Note that both these supply curves are short run. They assume that the wage, once set, is not adjusted in response to prices in the goods market. This shift produces excess demand just as surely as the new government-spending program did, only this time because the effective capacity of the economy has fallen. The economy used to be able to produce X at P_o, now it can produce only Y at a higher price level. Prices must rise to P_1, not to make room for increased government spending, but simply to distribute a smaller supply of goods.

It is not only labor demands that can produce these capacity reductions. An economy could depend heavily on imported inputs such as coal, oil, or steel. If the prices of imports rise, domestic businessmen must charge higher prices. A nation can become technically less productive over time. Its fixed capital may wear out, its supplies of natural resources may be exhausted, or it may have a bad agricultural harvest. Each of these causes a leftward shift in supply, excess demand at the previous period's prices, and inflation. Such inflation is caused by a fall in supply instead of a rise in demand.

The term wage, or cost-push, inflation seems to have gone out of style, although it is being revived. The reason is that it is so very difficult to determine the cause of the rise in nominal wages which moves the short-run supply curve to the left. This rise is quite likely to be justified by previous price increases. Walter Reuther's comments on that subject are quoted here.

The data reveal beyond all possibility of doubt that in each of the last three inflationary periods (including the current one), price increases preceded increases in labor costs. Moreover, the price increases were not necessitated by increases in other costs as indicated by the fact that, in each case, profits per unit of output were rising even before prices began to rise. The rises in unit labor costs began much later than the increases in prices—in the case of the current inflation, roughly 18 months later for manufacturing and later still for nonfinancial corporations.

Cost-Push Inflation

Figure 4.3

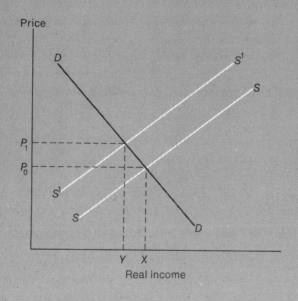

The increases in unit labor costs occurred primarily because of the workers' need to protect themselves and their families against erosion, resulting from *prior* price increases, of both their living standards and their share of the fruits of technological progress.

In other words, the indisputable evidence makes it clear that inflation was triggered, in each case, by corporations and not by workers. In each case, the thesis expressed by the late General Motors President, C. E. Wilson, as long ago as 1952, was borne out. Mr. Wilson wrote:

"I contend that we should not say 'the *wage*-price spiral.' We should say 'the *price*-wage spiral.' For it is not primarily wages that push up prices. It is primarily prices that *pull* up wages." [emphasis in original][2]

A glance at Figures 4.4 and 4.5 bears Reuther out. The rise in labor costs has come after the rise in prices. Our interpretation would be that it is a delayed reaction by labor to unexpected inflation during the early stages of a boom.

Previewing the argument of the following chapter, we are suggesting that there is a predictable sequence of shifts in the demand and supply curves during the typical inflation. First the demand curve shifts out, generally because of an increase in government expenditure. Labor's reaction to the initial price increase is a delayed demand for wage adjustments. This causes a leftward shift in the short-run supply curve and in the rising wages and prices, which have been labeled cost-push inflation. But if we are correct, this cost-push phase is related to or caused by the preceding demand-pull phase. It makes little sense to speak of rising wages as the cause of the rise in prices. In Chapter 5 we will analyze this inflationary process.

Questions

1. Define (a) cost-push inflation and (b) demand-pull inflation. Is it useful to distinguish between the two?

---

[2] Letter to economists from Walter Reuther, dated December 18, 1969. Reprinted by permission of United Automobile Workers.

Prices* and Labor Costs†

Figure 4.4

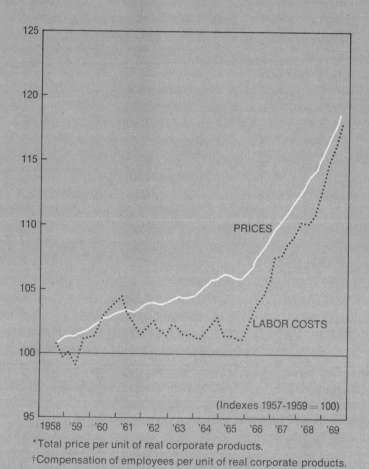

PRICES

LABOR COSTS

(Indexes 1957-1959 = 100)

*Total price per unit of real corporate products.
†Compensation of employees per unit of real corporate products.
SOURCE: *Survey of Current Business*, U. S. Department of Commerce.

Prices* and Profits
Before Taxes†

Figure 4.5

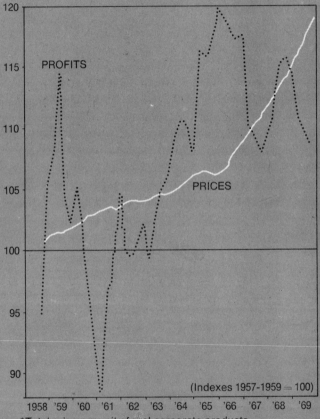

PROFITS

PRICES

(Indexes 1957-1959 = 100)

1958 '59 '60 '61 '62 '63 '64 '65 '66 '67 '68 '69

*Total price per unit of real corporate products.
†Corporate profits and inventory valuation of real corporate
products (does not include inventory profits resulting from
rising prices).

SOURCE: Survey of Current Business, U. S. Department of Commerce

2. We usually expect rising prices to force interest rates up, and thus to reduce investment expenditures. Yet the extremely high interest rates of the late 1960s failed, in general, to curtail investment expenditures. Can this apparent contradiction be explained by our theory?

3. Many writers have argued that the government should keep the unemployment level low by following full-employment policies which generate mild but beneficial inflations. Is this a feasible policy?

4. a) Discuss why the aggregate demand (*AD*) curve is downward sloping, while the aggregate supply (*AS*) curve is upward sloping.

   b) Why could we not derive the *AD* and the *AS* curves by summing the demand curves of all individuals and the supply of all firms?

5. Is it necessary to distinguish between "high" and "rising" rates of inflation? Does this distinction have any important implications for our analysis?

6. Suppose wages are rising faster than prices in an industry. Can you conclude from this that a cost-push inflation is in progress?

Suggestions for Further Reading

Dicks-Mireaux, L. A., and J. C. R. Dow, "The Interrelationship Between Cost and Price Changes, 1946–1959: A Study of Inflation in Postwar Britain," *Oxford Economic Papers* (October 1961), 267–292.

Dow, J. C. R., "Analysis of the Generation of Price Inflation," *Oxford Economic Papers* (October 1956), 252–301.

Holtzman, Franklyn D., "Inflation: Cost Push and Demand Pull," *American Economic Review* (March 1960), 20–42.

Phelps, Edmund, "A Test for the Presence of Cost Inflation in the United States, 1955–57," *Yale Economic Essays* (Spring 1961), 28–69.

Samuelson, Paul, and Robert Solow, "Analytical Aspects of Anti-Inflationary Policy," *American Economic Review, Proceedings* (May 1960), 177–194.

Selden, Richard T., "Cost Push vs. Demand Pull Inflation, 1955–57," *Journal of Political Economy* (February 1959), 1–20.

5
CHAPTER

A Description
of the
Inflationary Process

We now have a picture of how prices, wages, and output are determined period by period, and are ready to put these analyses together. This is where we will paste together into a kind of movie the still pictures we have been collecting of the inflationary process. Ours will be a multiperiod analysis in which the feedback mechanism, the link between periods, will be labor's reaction to previous forecasting errors. We use an exogenous shift in government expenditure as an example of an outside shock which generates an inflation. We will see how the economy makes a gradual adjustment in output and price to the change in demand conditions. Inflation is the name we give to the disequilibrium adjustment process. As will be seen, the simple model we have been developing generates a price-output path for the economy remarkably like that actually produced by the United States since 1960. Thus actual experience tends to confirm the model.

Adjustment to Excess Demand with No Expected Inflation

The dynamic analysis we are going to present amounts to a prediction of shifts in the aggregate demand and supply curves over time. On the demand side we assume that shifts in the demand curve are determined outside our model, that they are exogenous to it. We concentrate on the supply side, where our model implies predictable shifts in the aggregate supply over time.

There are two reasons for shifts in supply. The first is technological. Over time new machines are built, and the labor force becomes more skilled. This is what economists call technical change. All these factors make a given labor force more productive over time. Because the aggregate supply curve is derived by asking how much output the employed labor force can produce, technical change will be shifting this supply curve out over time.

The second reason why aggregate supply can shift is changes in expected prices by the labor force. In Chapter 3 we showed how a rise in the expected rate of inflation shifted the labor supply curve to the left. Translated to the goods market, a rise in expected inflation shifts the aggregate supply curve of the economy to the left. By the same reasoning a fall in expected inflation shifts the supply to the right. The reason is that the change in expectations changes the terms on which the unemployed can be hired.

Let us start our economy in a period of postinflationary recession with high unemployment and a negligible rate of inflation. In the first period the interaction of supply and demand in the goods market determines aggregate income and the price level. Why is unemployment in the recession abnormally high? It is high because the actual rate of inflation is less than the unemployed thought it would be. They demand nominal wages beyond what business is willing to pay, because they expect prices to rise. When the actual rate of inflation is less than they had expected, they are temporarily unemployed; but they also adjust their rate of inflation downward. In the following period the nominal wages required to hire the unemployed will be lower, and the aggregate supply curve of the economy will have shifted to the right.

It may be useful to introduce a diagram of the economy to illustrate the process of change we are analyzing. Because we are going to follow the process over time, we must date our demand and our supply curves. S_2 lies to the right of S_1, both

Goods Market Equilibrium during Periods 1, 2, and 3

Figure 5.1

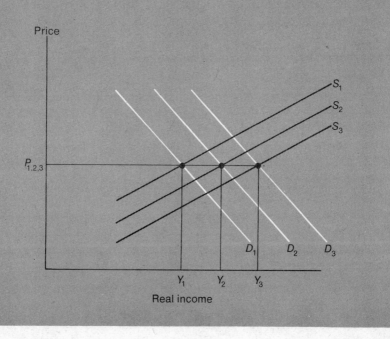

because of the downward adjustment of expected inflation (remember that this is an economy in a postinflationary recession) and because of technological change.

Now consider demand. Suppose that in period 2 the government decides to engage in new spending programs. It may build roads or rockets, enlarge subsidies, or lower taxes. In all cases the aggregate demand curve of the economy shifts to the right, as shown in Figure 5.1. As we have portrayed the shifts, the increase in what we could call effective capacity is just enough to offset the increase in demand. Output and employment rise, but there is no induced inflation.

Suppose that during period 3 the multiplier effects of the government programs continue to work themselves out. Businessmen find that their profits have risen and previously unemployed workers now have jobs, so disposable income of both labor and management has risen during period 2. Hence private consumption expenditures rise during period 3. The demand curve shifts still further to the right. Let us suppose that during period 3 the actual price level coincides exactly with expectations. As we found in Chapter 3, this implies that the economy is on its long-run supply curve. Unemployment is at its "normal" or long-run frictional level. At this point there will be no further expectations adjustments in the aggregate supply curve. From now on, noninflationary growth in output is possible only to the extent that the supply curve continues to move out because of technical change.

During period 4, suppose that, just as the government is congratulating itself on the success of its anti-inflation program, it is confronted with the necessity of increased spending. The most obvious example might be a war, but any sudden jump in private sector demand would have the same effect. Ideally the government should raise taxes or reduce other spending programs of its own at this point, but let us suppose that it does not. The result is another rightward shift in aggregate demand. But the economy no longer has idle machines or idle men to supply the additional output being demanded by the government. Businessmen can increase output by hiring more labor, but the real product of extra laborers is falling. To offset the resultant loss in real product (MPP), business must either be able to pay lower nominal wages or raise its own selling prices. It cannot hire men at lower wages, because no one is willing to work at a lower real wage than that implied by the preceding year's nominal wage and price levels. So prices rise. This enables businessmen to increase output and employment. Remember that this works only so long as nominal wages of employed workers are unaffected by the change in prices, that is, under our assumption that labor does not perceive the change in prices. What we see in period 4 is the start of an inflation. As the reader can see from Figure 5.2, the shift in demand $D_4 D_4$ causes output to rise to Y_4. But now for the first time there is inflation.

$$\frac{P_4}{P_3} > 1$$

In period 5 the government is faced with a decision. Should it cut off the incipient boom by reduced spending, or should it bask in the optimism generated by high levels of employment and output after the previous years of stagnation and recession? Let us suppose that it goes the latter route, and maintains its period 4 expenditure levels. Although government demand has leveled off, private sector spending increases, because of the delayed multiplier effects of the period 4 increase in government spending. This means that once again the aggregate demand curve shifts to the right.

Now for the first time in our process, labor reacts to unforeseen price changes and demands an increase in nominal wages to offset period 4 inflation. As we have shown in Chapter 3, this tends to reduce the capacity of the economy and to shift aggregate supply to the left. Suppose that this shift just offsets the outward shift in supply caused by continued technical change so that the supply curves of periods 4 and 5 coincide. To summarize the situation, as shown in Figure 5.2, output and employment rise once again, although at a slower rate than before, and the inflation accelerates. The economy is apparently in the middle of a demand-pull inflation.

In period 6 the government decides to take action against the inflation by reducing its expenditures. This shifts the aggregate demand curve to the left. But the action does not stop the inflation, because supply conditions are still changing in

Goods Market Equilibrium during Periods 4 and 5

Figure 5.2

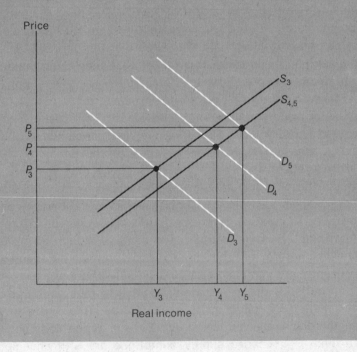

an inflationary way. Labor again discovers that it has misforecast inflation, and nominal wage demands are raised accordingly. Assume that the expectations adjustment dominates technical change so that the aggregate supply shifts to the left. Whether or not the outcome is higher or lower prices depends on whether nominal wages adjusted for technical change have risen faster or slower than demand has fallen. To put it another way, inflation will be stopped if demand falls more than effective capacity. As we have drawn it in Figure 5.3, the inflation continues, because the government is unable to reduce demand as fast as effective capacity is falling.

We can see that if supply conditions were to remain unchanged $(S_5 = S_4)$, period 6 equilibrium would have lower output and prices. The inflation would be stopped. But because there was an unexpected inflation during period 5, it is unrealistic to suppose that the effective supply curve remains in its period 5 position. By experimenting with various hypothetical period 5 supply curves, the reader can see that so long as S_6 lies further to the left of S_5 than D_6 lies from D_5, prices continue to rise. Output falls regardless. What we are saying is that if effective capacity in the economy falls faster than demand, there will be excess demand at the previous price level, and prices must rise.

At the beginning of a stabilization it is highly likely that supply will be falling faster than demand. How far does the supply curve shift? Remember that the shift is caused by a rise in nominal wage demanded by workers less the rate of technical progress. If last year's inflation was 4 percent and there is a 2 percent annual increase in productivity, labor will be asking for 6 percent higher wages, 4 percent to offset the inflation and 2 percent for technical change. In order to supply the same quantity of goods, the typical factory must raise its selling prices by 4 percent. In other words the supply curve should be 4 percent higher at the previous year's output level. While this is not the same as the curve having shifted to the *left* by 4 percent, it will not be too far wrong to think of supply as shifting to the left each year at about the rate of the previous year's inflation.

The demand curve will probably be making much smaller shifts. Generally, stabilization programs are gradual and mean

Goods Market Equilibrium in Period 6

Figure 5.3

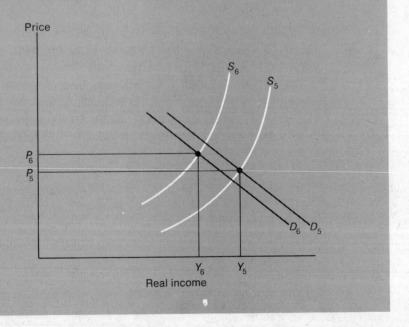

only that previous rates of growth in government spending are halted. It is not likely that a government would knowingly reduce aggregate demand by 4 percent in response to a 4 percent inflation the previous year. The most likely stabilization sequence is a series of leftward shifts in supply greater than in demand, and therefore rising prices and falling output.

We have drawn the period 6 supply and demand curves to represent a gradual stabilization in which there is a small reduction in demand in relation to the reduction in capacity or supply. Prices continue to rise during the period, but now, for the first time, output falls. This rise in prices appears to be a result of the reduction in effective capacity due to wage demands. For this reason this phase of the inflation used to be labeled cost-push. Wages rise faster than prices, and output falls—all the classic symptoms of a cost-push inflation. But if our description of the process is accurate, the wage demands in period 6 were caused by the inflation in period 5, which was caused ultimately by the increase in government expenditures in period 4. In other words the phase of an inflation when prices and wages are increasing and output is falling cannot really be separated and labeled. It is the stabilization phase of an inflationary process which was initiated by excess demand. In the new equilibrium, both prices and wages will have adjusted to the new conditions. But if we are right in our assumption that labor reacts to price changes with a lag, the adjustment in wages and prices is not simultaneous. Instead, there are two phases, the first when prices are increasing while labor is being fooled by inflation, and the second when prices and wages are both reacting. Typically in the first phase, output and employment are expanding, because the rise in nominal wages then occurring is taken by labor to be an equivalent rise in real wages. The extra production which occurs during that part of the process is in some sense involuntary. It would not have occurred had labor been fully aware of price trends. The second phase of the process is the correction of these mistaken price forecasts by labor and the elimination of involuntary overemployment and production. Wages and prices continue to rise and output falls. This is the stabilization phase, an integral and unavoidable part of the entire process which follows from erroneous price forecasts.

The reader should ask himself what the adjustment to excess demand would be like if nominal wages reacted instantaneously to price changes. We have already seen that this would make it impossible to increase output through inflation. An economy might have an inflation, but there would be no boom in real output or employment. Rising prices would serve only to redistribute a constant amount of total goods among the various buyers in the economy. More germane to our point, if the wage and price adjustments were instantaneous and simultaneous, the entire price adjustment would occur immediately and there could be no talk of demand-pull or cost-push inflation. It is only in a world of imperfect foresight or, equivalently, sticky wages that this adjustment requires a number of periods and involves the kinds of feedbacks between inflation and wages that we have been describing.

One could say that imperfect foresight allows the economy to have its total inflation on the installment plan. As we know, the long-run economy supply curve is vertical. A shift outward in demand by the government is going to result in an increase in prices great enough to reduce private spending by the same amount as the multiplier times the new government-spending program. Thus the total amount of inflation is constant. With imperfect foresight it is undergone over a number of periods instead of all at once, as it would be under perfect foresight. Employment and output temporarily exceed their long-run levels. Far from blaming labor for excessive wage demands during the stabilization phase, the public should be happy it did not have the inflation sooner.

Effect of Expected Inflation on the Adjustment Process

We left our hypothetical economy in period 6 in the unpleasant situation of an inflation in prices and a recession in output—the worst of all possible worlds, it would appear. But more unpleasant news may still be in store for the economy. So far, labor has been acting as if its inflationary expectations are zero. It has been demanding wage increases solely to compensate for previous inflation. In period 6, nominal wages demanded rose by the amount of period 5 inflation. Labor was

74

acting as if it expected no further inflation during period 6. Labor was deflating nominal wages by a period 5 price index. But prices did increase during period 6, so that workers actually were working for less than planned real wages. At some point in an inflation, labor is likely to begin to anticipate inflation. When it does, nominal wage demands will be rising by enough to offset both previous inflation and expected future inflation. In other words, when labor begins to expect inflation, nominal wage increases become greater than before, and this implies a larger reduction in the effective capacity of the economy than before. In diagrammatic terms the aggregate supply curve shifts to the left by more than it did before.

The government is now faced with an unpleasant choice. If it continues with its stabilization program, there will be a large increase in unemployment and a deepening of the recession. If it allows demand to increase, the inflation will be even worse. In figure 5.4 we have drawn a large leftward shift in supply during period 7 to reflect the shift to positive expected inflation. As the reader can see, if aggregate demand is simply held constant, output will fall to Y_7, which implies an increase in unemployment of all the workers who would have been required to produce the output that is being foregone ($Y_6 - Y_7$). If the government is worried by this increase in unemployment, it might increase its spending. It can hold output constant by allowing demand to increase to the dotted line $\hat{D}_7$, but that will further aggravate the inflation. Instead of having price increases of $P_7 - P_6$, the economy would have $\hat{P}_7 - P_6$.

Let us suppose that the government manages its affairs so as to hold demand in period 7 at demand curve D_6—meaning that it holds nominal demand constant, so that any increase in prices will result in a fall in real purchases. (If it were to hold demand constant in real terms, the aggregate demand curve would be vertical.) Once again output falls and the rate of inflation may even accelerate, depending on how much the supply curve has shifted. At this point there will surely be complaints that the government stabilization policy is ineffective. Price and wage controls will be suggested, because it appears that the restrictive government-spending plan has resulted in a recession in employment and output, with no noticeable effect on the inflation.

Goods Market Equilibrium in Period 7

Figure 5.4

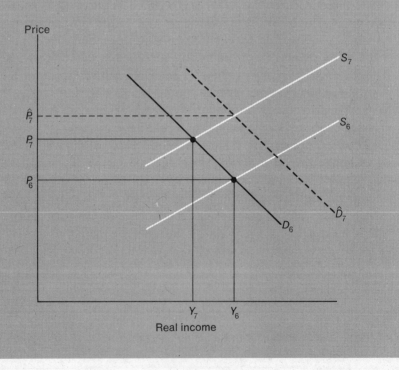

The switch to positive inflationary expectations by labor is a crucial turning point during the stabilization phase. So long as labor is simply reacting to previous actual inflation, it is possible to reach a new equilibrium price level in a relatively painless way. Involuntary overemployment is gradually eliminated as real wages approach their equilibrium level, but there is no involuntary underemployment.

Once expectations of future inflation are positive, it is no longer true that the total inflation in response to an initial increase in demand is constant, nor can price stability be reached without a period of involuntary unemployment. The reason involuntary overemployment exists during the expansion phase is because of an artificial drop in the real wage at which labor is willing to work. But with positive expectations about future price changes, the actual real wage will be at the full employment level only if the expected rate of inflation materializes. During a stabilization program the aim of the government is precisely to reduce actual inflation below the expected level. If it succeeds, therefore, the real wage will be above the long-run equilibrium level, which means that there will be involuntary unemployment. Since the government has not yet found any way to reduce expected inflation except by making the actual inflation less than expected, stabilization is going to mean a period of high, involuntary unemployment whenever labor's rate of expected inflation is greater than that acceptable to government.

We need not continue our period analysis in such great detail. After the onset of positive inflationary expectations, the government has the choice of holding demand constant and incurring high unemployment or ratifying those expectations by allowing demand to expand at the rate necessary to equalize actual inflation and expected inflation. In that case employment and output stabilize at their long-run levels, but with a permanent inflation. This is probably what has occurred in several Latin American countries. Expectations about inflation have become so firmly positive that the cost of reducing them is a very long period of stagnation and above-normal unemployment. Rather than pay that cost, several Latin American governments have adjusted the financial and tax systems to a permanent inflation. It is not clear that this is an unwise policy decision.

When the government holds demand constant, there is an adjustment period during which prices continue to rise, although at a rate less than that expected by labor. Employment and output are below normal levels. Eventually this involuntary unemployment stops further wage increases, and a new equilibrium is reached. How long the process takes is an open question; it depends on how long it takes to drive expectations about inflation back to an acceptable level. So long as they are above that level, price stability cannot be achieved without foregoing a high sacrifice in unemployment and output. It is small wonder that the United States government so firmly and continuously announces its intention of stopping our inflation. If this sort of verbal warfare helps damp the expectations of future inflation, it is useful and self-fulfilling.

Comparison of the Hypothetical Inflation Process and Actual Inflations

The hypothetical sequence of employment, output, and price change we have described corresponds quite closely with recent United States experience. Arthur Okun, in a recent informative book, describes the process by which the United States got into a serious inflation during the last half of the 1960s.[1] We came out of the 1950s with substantial excess capacity and unemployment, which were the result of a long stabilization period after the Korean War inflation. President John F. Kennedy was determined to get the country "moving again," and he proceeded to do this by increasing government expenditure and cutting personal income taxes. By 1964 or 1965 we were back at so-called full employment. At just that moment the United States became enmeshed in a costly war in Vietnam. We no longer had the excess capacity in men or machines to supply the extra output required by that conflict. For reasons that will be debated by the historians, there was no effective reduction in demand elsewhere until about 1968, when the tax

---

[1] Arthur M. Okun, *The Political Economy of Prosperity*. (New York: Norton, 1970).

surcharge went into effect. The result was the worst inflation since the Korean War. The hypothetical scenario we used to generate our inflationary process corresponds closely with this actual set of events.

One way to compare the theoretical and the actual results is to look at price and output in the goods market over time. Keep in mind that all we ever observe are intersections of supply and demand curves. We have an idea what the curves should look like, but we never observe them. Our theoretical analysis leads us to expect a certain sequence of supply curve shifts which imply that the actual intersection points will behave in a definite predictable way. By comparing our prediction with the actual event, we can test our theory of the inflationary process.

Figure 5.5 shows all the supply and demand curves that we have developed for the various periods described. The subscripts, as before, refer to the period. Since equilibrium in any period is the intersection of supply and demand, one finds it by looking at the intersection of supply and demand curves with the same numerical subscript. Each intersection is marked with a dot. From period 6 on, the demand curve is constant.

The process as we have described it traces a counter-clockwise cyclic movement in real income. Starting from the initial recession, the economy has a period of expansion in output with no inflation. Then as demand continues to rise, there is a period of what used to be called demand-pull inflation. Output and prices are both increasing. We have called this phase of the inflation the expansionary phase. It includes periods 4 and 5. Eventually, demand stops rising fast enough to offset the leftward shifts in supply, and output begins to fall, even though prices continue to rise. Because demand is no longer rising, we have called this phase of the inflation the stabilization phase. It includes periods 6 and 7 in our diagram. Successive equilibrium points now move northwest on our diagram, instead of northeast.

Thus the typical inflation should move through the sequence of output-price combinations shown in Figure 5.6. Let us compare this with the actual United States experience in the 1950s and 1960s. In Figure 5.7 we plot real GNP against the GNP price index for the relevant years. As can be seen, the typical coun-

79

Goods Market Equilibrium during an Inflation

Figure 5.5

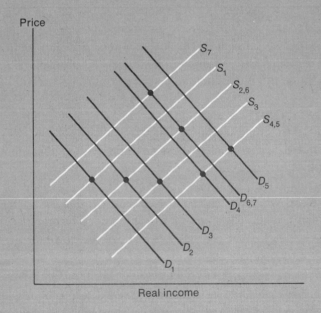

Typical Inflation–Output Pattern

Figure 5.6

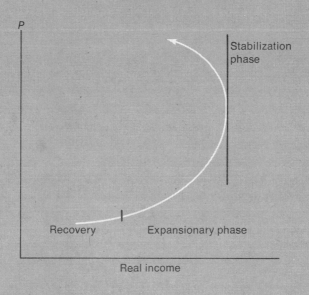

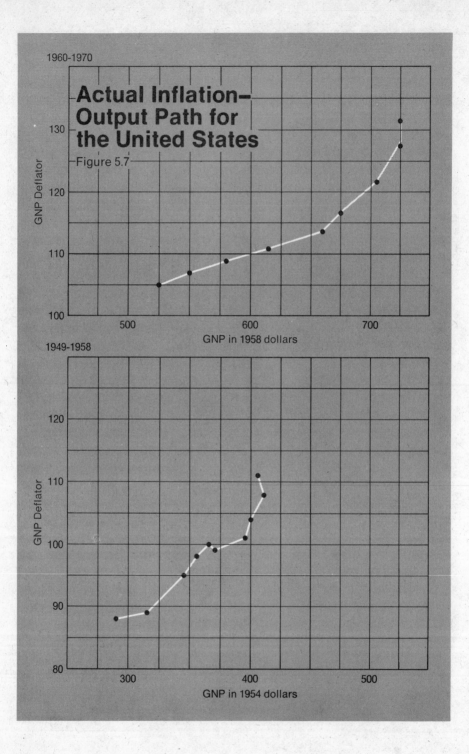

Actual Inflation–
Output Path for
the United States
Figure 5.7

1960-1970

1949-1958

GNP Deflator

GNP in 1958 dollars

GNP in 1954 dollars

terclockwise movement predicted by our model is confirmed for both inflations. The pattern is somewhat distorted by price controls during the Korean War, but one can view the late 1950s as the stabilization phase of the Korean War-World War inflations. Analysts and economists invented the term cost-push inflation to describe the period, but if one accepts our theory that stabilization and preceding expansion cannot be separated, the late 1950s were the inevitable result of previous war-generated excess demand. More relevant to today, by 1969 the economy had moved into the stabilization phase of the 1960s inflation. Output is falling, unemployment is rising, and so still are prices. It is an uncomfortable world for economic policy makers, as all stabilizations are. With the 1950s as a guide, the stabilization is unlikely to be short or painless. All the evidence suggests that inflationary expectations are strongly positive, so that a number of years of high unemployment and low output levels will be required to reverse them. Clearly the more gradual the program is (the less the demand curve falls), the longer the stabilization will take.

The Trade-off between Output and Employment

One of our principal contentions in this book is that the expansionary and stabilization phases of an inflation are related, that they are part of a single process. It follows from this that there is no permanent trade-off between output and inflation. Proponents of an expansionary policy used to say that one could buy extra output and employment by a little bit of inflation. But they were looking at the expansionary phase only, and were forgetting the inevitable stabilization. You could say that they were taking the short-run point of view. In the short run, as we have seen, higher prices do bring more output and employment, but only because the price increases are not anticipated. During the ensuing stabilization phase, all the extra output is eliminated as labor adjusts to new price levels. At best the inflation brings a temporary increase in output and employment.

In the long run, the capacity of the economy is determined by the productivity of the labor force. Capacity is fixed by these technical factors; it is not influenced by prices. As we have seen, the long-run aggregate supply curve is vertical and shifts outward over time. In the short run the economy can get off the long-run curve, because wage adjustments to price changes are not instantaneous, meaning that, temporarily, higher prices produce more output. Eventually the economy must return to its long-run curve, meaning that all the extra output above that produced by changes in productivity is eliminated. If throughout the entire inflation labor never acts as if it expected inflation, the situation can be depicted as in Figure 5.8. High prices result in a temporary income bulge, but the permanent result is simply higher prices.

The situation changes fundamentally if expectations by labor adjust to the inflation. When labor expects future price increases and adjusts nominal wages accordingly, price stability can be achieved only by a period during which actual inflation is less than expected inflation. During that period real wages are greater than their long-run level, while employment and output fall below their long-run rates. In other words, with positive expected inflation during the inflationary process, there must be a period during which the economy is to the left of the long-run supply curve. Then we have the S-shaped movement around the long-run supply curve shown in Figure 5.9. During the expansion phase there is a temporary northeasterly movement (that is, above-normal output with unexpected rising prices). This is followed by a fall to less than normal output with still higher prices. With positive expected inflation, we no longer get just a temporary bulge in output. Now the extra output is balanced by a later short fall. The trade-off is not between inflation and output, but between output now and output later. Higher than normal output during the expansionary phase is counterbalanced by lower than normal output during the stabilization phase.

As Milton Friedman has put it:

> There is always a temporary trade-off between inflation and unemployment; there is no permanent trade-off. The temporary trade-off comes not from inflation per se, but from unanticipated inflation, which generally means from a rising rate of inflation. The widespread belief that there is a permanent trade-off is a sophisticated version of the confusion between "high" and

Zero Expected Inflation

Figure 5.8

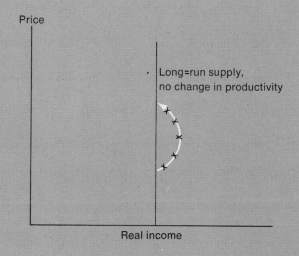

Price

Long=run supply,
no change in productivity

Real income

Positive Expected Inflation

Figure 5.9

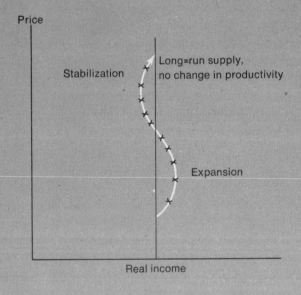

"rising" that we all recognize in simpler forms. A rising rate of inflation may reduce unemployment, a high rate will not.[2]

If expectations are slow to adapt to unexpected inflation, an inflationary policy can produce temporary above-normal output and employment. All our experience in the 1960s, however, shows quite clearly that labor has adapted rapidly to rising prices. Labor contracts currently being signed reflect strongly positive expected future inflation. Thus the inflation-output trade-off in the United States economy is most likely to be of the more-now, less-later variety. Inflation is not a very appealing policy for increasing GNP and employment.

Questions

1. How might the cyclic pattern of output and prices be different in economies with slow and fast adjustments of expectations to inflation?
2. What would happen to the cycle we have described if all contracts had cost of living escalators?
3. a) Given an inflationary pattern as described in this chapter, what anti-inflationary policies do you think the government should follow?
   b) What would you expect the results of these policies to be on employment and output?
   c) At what point during the inflation do you think the government should institute its anti-inflationary policies?

Suggestions for Further Reading

Ball, R. J., *Inflation and the Theory of Money*. Chicago: Aldine, 1965.

---

[2] Milton Friedman, "The Role of Monetary Policy," *American Economic Review* (March 1968).

Bresciani-Turroni, C., *The Economics of Inflation.* London: Kelley, 1937.

Haggar, A. J., *The Theory of Inflation.* Melbourne: Melbourne University Press, 1964.

Hansen, Bent, *A Study in the Theory of Inflation.* London: Kelley, 1951.

Koopmans, Tjaeling C., "Dynamics of Inflation," *Review of Economics and Statistics* (May 1942), 53–65.

Okun, Arthur M., *The Political Economy of Prosperity.* New York; W. W. Norton, 1970.

Schultze, Charles, Study Paper No. 1 in Joint Economic Committee, *Recent Inflation in the United States* (Washington, D. C., 1959).

Turvey, Ralph, "Some Aspects of the Theory of Inflation in a Closed Economy," *Economic Journal* (September 1951), 532–543.

Weintraub, Sidney, *A General Theory of the Price Level, Output, Income Distribution and Economic Growth.* Philadelphia; Chilton Book Company, 1959.

6
CHAPTER

The
Phillips
Curve

It appears to be an empirical fact that when rates of unemployment are high, the rate of change of prices and wages is low, and vice versa. This suggests that there is a trade-off between unemployment and inflation or wage changes, which has prompted an enormous amount of research into the exact nature and stability of the trade-off. A. W. Phillips, one of the earliest investigators, plotted actual unemployment rates against wage changes for Great Britain from 1861 to 1957 and noticed that over each cycle the resulting points traced a rounded L-shaped curve. This same relation, now known as the Phillips curve, has been confirmed for the United States and extended to price changes as well as to wage changes.

Figure 6.1 summarizes the United States experience.

When we plot money wage rates against the rate of unemployment, we get a curve which seems to be roughly stable over time. Stop and think what this implies. If the curve is stable, an economy would seem to have the choice of operating at low employment-low inflation or high employment-high inflation. It would seem that the existence of the Phillips curve relation means that a trade-off between inflation and employment is possible after all.

The Phillips Curve

Figure 6.1

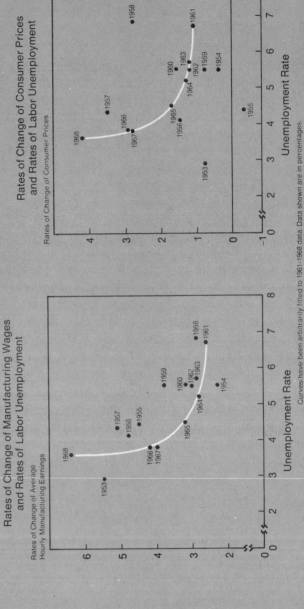

Rates of Change of Manufacturing Wages
and Rates of Labor Unemployment

Rates of Change of Average
Hourly Manufacturing Earnings

Rates of Change of Consumer Prices
and Rates of Labor Unemployment

Rates of Change of Consumer Prices

Unemployment Rate

Unemployment Rate

SOURCE: Roger W. Spencer. "The Relation Between Prices and Employment: Two Views." Federal Reserve Bank of St. Louis *Review.* (March 1969).

Curves have been arbitrarily fitted to 1961-1968 data. Data shown are in percentages.

90

If our view of the inflationary process is correct, the Phillips curve is a natural result of labor's erroneous short-run price forecasts. We will show that each short-run Phillips curve corresponds to a particular expected rate of inflation. As the expected rate of inflation rises during a period of rising prices, the economy actually shifts from one short-run curve to another. The reason we seem to have had only one curve in the past is that periods of high inflation have been followed by stabilizations before price expectations had time to adjust fully. One could say that if the Phillips curve had been used for policy in the past, it would not have been observed. Let us go into these points in more detail.

Phillips Curve as a Result of Erroneous Price Forecasts

In Chapter 3 on the labor market we were concerned with the determination of equilibrium employment and real wage levels. Now our attention is focused on unemployment, the other side of the employment coin. The U. S. Department of Labor defines an unemployed as one actively seeking work, but not working. That is, the unemployed are members of the labor force who are devoting full time to searching for jobs. In terms of the labor market diagram (Figure 6.2), unemployment is the difference between employment and the labor force, or $L_f - L_e$. Recall how we showed in Chapter 3 that whenever the rate of inflation was different from what it was expected to be, the actual supply curve of people willing to work, S_a, was different from the perceived supply curve, S_p. If the rate of inflation was greater than expected, S_a was to the right of S_p; if it was less, S_a lay to the left of S_p. When the rate was exactly equal to expectations, unemployment was at the long-run, normal frictional level. In terms of unemployment, this is equivalent to saying that when the actual rate of inflation is greater than expected, the level of unemployment is less than normal, and vice versa—exactly what the Phillips curve shows.

Let us trace a Phillips curve, using the hypothetical labor market example of Chapter 3. We are going to show how an increase in the rate of inflation will reduce unemployment *so*

91

The Labor Market

Figure 6.2

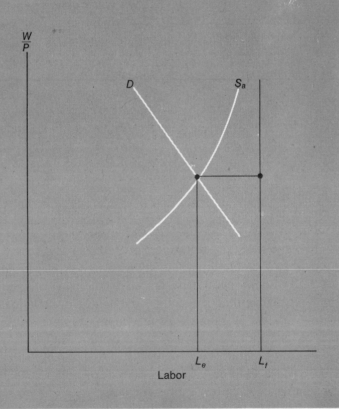

long as expected inflation is constant. For simplicity, suppose that labor expects no inflation. Wage increases demanded are solely for the purpose of catching up with inflation in prior years. The labor force is assumed to be constant at 1.3 million men.

TABLE 6.1

Hypothetical Wage, Price, Employment, and Unemployment in an Economy with Zero Expected Inflation

Period	Nominal Wage/Day	Price Index	Inflation	Real Wage	Employment (in millions)	Unemployment (in millions)
0	$10.00	100	0	$10.00	1.0	0.3
1	11.00	115	15	9.57	1.2	0.1
2	13.25	147	28	9.00	1.25	0.05
3	16.17	169	15	9.57	1.2	0.1
4	16.90	169	0	10.00	1.0	0.3

When we say that labor expects no inflation, we mean that it is deflating this period's wage offer by last period's price index. Whenever there is inflation, therefore, the actual supply curve will lie to the right of the perceived curve, and employment will be greater than normal.

In period 1, nominal wages rise by $1 per day. This increase reduces frictional unemployment by 0.2 million, even though there is a 15 percent rise in prices. Because the rise is unexpected, it enables the system to move out the short-run Phillips curve to point 1.

In period 2, labor demands a 15 percent increase in nominal wages to offset the unexpected loss in purchasing power during period 1. If there were no further rise in prices, the economy would return to point 0. But suppose that the inflationary process continues. The rate of inflation accelerates to 28 percent. The nominal wage rises by more than 15 percent, so that labor again believes that real wages have risen. The real wage as perceived by labor is $13.25/115 = 11.50. An increase in the rate of inflation to 28 percent reduces unemployment still further as the economy moves to point 2 on the Phillips curve in Figure 6.3.

93

Hypothetical Phillips Curve from Table 6.1

Figure 6.3

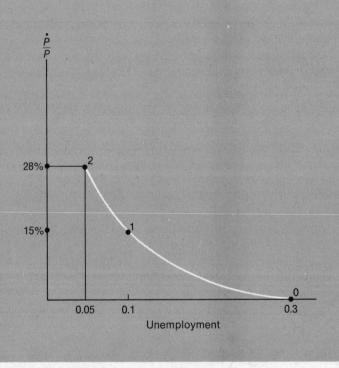

In period 3, we begin a deceleration of inflation. Labor demands a 28 percent increase in wages to compensate for the inflation in period 2. But prices rise by only 15 percent. Labor, believing that the real wage has increased to $11, again supplies 1.2 million men. The economy is moving back down the Phillips curve from point 2 to point 1. In the following period, with inflation eliminated, the inflationary reduction in real wages is overcome, because the inflation is finally reduced to its expected level. The economy moves back down the Phillips curve from point 1 to point 0.

Notice two things about this process. First, our model does trace a Phillips curve. Second, the curve does represent alternative possible states for the economy, so long as expected inflation is constant. The reader should be able to show that whenever the rate of inflation is 15 percent, the economy will be at point 1; whenever the rate is 28 percent, the economy will be at point 2.

The situation changes fundamentally when actual inflation leads people to expect more inflation. Then, as we have seen in Chapter 3, workers will demand wage increases, both for last year's inflation and for the further inflation expected this year. This demand will shift the entire short-run Phillips curve upward. In our example, suppose that during period 2, labor raises its expected inflation to the rate of the previous year. By the end of period 2, therefore, labor expects the price index to be 15 percent higher than it was the previous year. It deflates nominal wages by 132 (115 × 115). What then does the Phillips curve for 15 percent expected inflation look like? We know that if the actual inflation equals expected, employment will be at its normal level of 1 million men. Therefore the curve passes through point C in Figure 6.4.

To generate an unemployment rate of 0.1 million, we know that the perceived wage by labor must be $11 and that the actual real wage must be $9.57. Nominal wages must rise (during period 2) to $14.57 ($11 × 1.3225). But this means that prices must rise to 152 ($14.55 ÷ $9.57), a rate of inflation of 32.25 percent (152 ÷ 115). In other words the whole curve shifts up by 15 percent.

If there is a different short-run Phillips curve for every level of expected inflation, we can understand why the existence of

Effect of Changing Expectations on the Phillips Curve

Figure 6.4

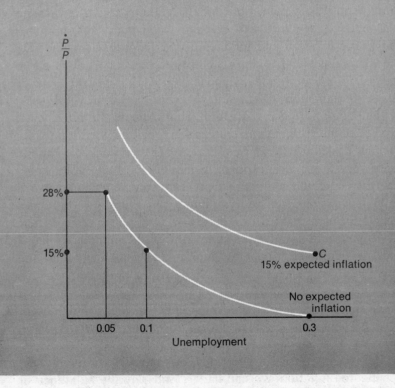

$\frac{\dot{P}}{P}$

28%

15%

C

15% expected inflation

No expected inflation

0.05   0.1   0.3

Unemployment

the short-run curve says nothing about the possibility of a trade-off between inflation and unemployment. For one must expect labor to react to unexpected inflation by adjusting its rate of inflation upward. Thus, whenever the economy moves to the left up a short-run curve, it will tend to move vertically above the curve to higher curves as expectations adjust.

But the reader may protest, how can we say that the inflation-unemployment trade-off is not possible when historically the economy has actually moved out a short-run Phillips curve? Suppose that you are a government economist, and you have found a stable Phillips curve relation which indicates that the economy has the following alternatives:

Unemployment (rate)	Change in Wages (rate)	Inflation (rate)
3%	3%	2%
4	2	0
5	1	−2

The 2 percent increase in real wages which occurs at 4 percent is the result of increases in technical efficiency of labor over time, owing to additions to the capital stock. Now suppose the economy has actually moved from the 4 percent unemployment and stable price combination to the 3 percent unemployment with 2 percent inflation on several different previous occasions. Would you not be tempted to present the two positions as alternatives and argue that you could reduce unemployment by 1 percent at the cost of 2 percent inflation?

The government may view 2 percent inflation as a cheap price to pay for a 1 percent reduction in unemployment, and proceed to adopt expansionary fiscal policy to achieve the 2 percent inflation. In period 1, nominal wages rise by 3 percent instead of the customary 2 percent. Prices also rise, although this is unexpected by labor. Labor thinks that real wages have risen by 3 percent instead of 2 percent, while business realizes that wages have risen 1 percent rather then 2 percent. The result is that employment and output rise and unemployment falls. The government has reached point *A* on the short-run

Phillips curve. But unfortunately for government, this is not the end of the story. In period 2, labor reacts to the unexpected 2 percent inflation. Unemployment dropped in period 1, because labor thought that it was receiving a 1 percent larger than normal increase in its real wage. But in fact its real wage rose by only 1 percent. To make up for this unexpected loss, labor will therefore demand its usual 2 percent nominal wage boost plus 2 percent for the unexpected inflation in period 1 plus a further increase to offset whatever inflation it has learned to expect. In order to hold unemployment at the 3 percent level, the government finds that nominal wages must rise by more than 3 percent. But businessmen cannot maintain the high employment level unless the actual real wage stays at the period 1 level. This means that inflation has to be greater than 2 percent. The government has to allow the inflation to accelerate in order to maintain the desired 3 percent employment rate. The trade-off seems to be evaporating as the economy moves to point *B* on a new Phillips curve, Figure 6.5.

As soon as labor begins to expect future inflation and to demand wage increases to make up not only for past price changes but also for future ones, the rate of wage and price change required to maintain the 3 percent level of unemployment accelerates. As the history of unexpected inflation lengthens, this adaptation of expectations is bound to occur. Thus the government finds itself pursuing an unviable policy. Instead of having brought a 1 percent reduction in unemployment with 2 percent inflation, it has put the economy into an ever-worsening inflation for so long as it attempts to maintain the 3 percent unemployment level. This is because the 3 percent rate of unemployment is not at an equilibrium level. The economy achieves it in the short run only because of differences between what labor perceives the real wage to be and what it actually is. Each year, as labor adjusts to previous forecasting errors, greater and greater inflation is required just to maintain the same employment. The economy has to run harder and harder just to stand still.

Our analysis implies that it is not possible for the economy to stay permanently at any point on the short-run Phillips curve except at the long-run natural rate of unemployment. When

Movements on the Phillips Curve

Figure 6.5

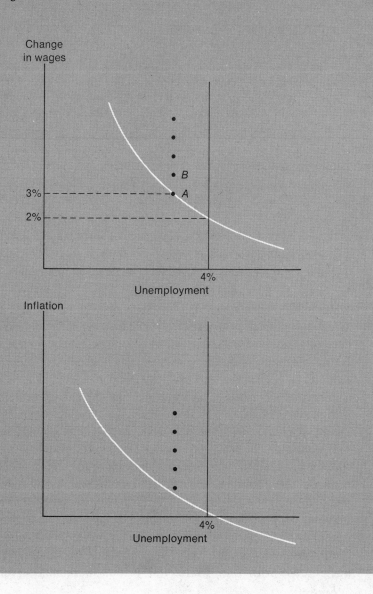

the government tries to reach any other point and stay at that point, there is a gradually accelerating upward movement above the short-run curve. Here, then, is the answer to the puzzle of why the Phillips curve does not represent viable alternative states of the economy, even though the economy is generally on the curve. The curve is traced during the normal boom-recession inflationary cycle. Expansion historically has always been followed by stabilization. The cycle has reversed the upward adjustment of expectations, so that the economy has remained, more or less, on one curve. You could say, therefore, that the short-run curve is observable for actual economies exactly because it has never been used as the basis for policy making. When a government attempts to move an economy out a short-run curve away from the normal unemployment level, there is a gradual (or perhaps not so gradual) upward movement of the whole curve as the economy adjusts to unexpected inflation. Under such a policy one would not observe the short-run curve. One cannot use the observed Phillips curve as an indicator of the trade-off between inflation and unemployment.

With this analysis in mind, let us observe recent United States experience. What is our so-called natural rate of unemployment? There is no way to know exactly what such a rate is, because it could occur with any combination of nominal wage and price changes. We do know, however, that departures from the rate should generate substantial inflationary or deflationary pressure. Among economists there is some consensus that 4 percent unemployment must be close to this natural rate.

Accepting this, let us refer to the United States inflation during the 1960s.

By perhaps 1965 the economy was at full employment by our definition, but the increased volume of military expenditures continued to generate demand. Inflation began to accelerate and the economy moved to less than normal unemployment. From 1965 through 1967 there seemed to be a trade-off between inflation and unemployment. Inflation rose from 1.7 percent to 2.9 percent in return for a reduction in unemployment from 4.5 percent to 3.8 percent. But the economy could not remain with that trade-off. Further increases in employ-

TABLE 6.2

Employment, Inflation, and Growth of GNP in the 1960s[1]

Year	Unemployment Rate	Real Rate of Growth	Rate of Inflation (CPI)
1964	5.2%	2.4%	1.3%
1965	4.5	3.0	1.7
1966	3.8	3.1	2.9
1967	3.8	1.5	2.8
1968	3.6	1.5	4.2
1969	3.5	1.3	5.4
1970	4.9	—0.1	5.7

ment became more and more expensive in terms of inflation. By 1969 it was clear that inflation was accelerating, even though there was no great further reduction in unemployment. To have maintained even the 3.5 percent rate of 1969 would have required a substantial increase in inflation, because labor was rapidly adjusting its expectations to an inflationary world. Wage settlements involving from 6 to 8 percent annual increases in future nominal wages were common. The government was forced to recognize that its 3.5 percent unemployment rate was not viable, because it implied accelerating inflation. It was therefore forced to stabilize. The early 1970s promise to be a painful adjustment to lower levels of inflation.

Short-Run versus Long-Run Phillips Curves

In the goods market analysis, we saw that there was a big difference between the short run and the long run. This same difference shows up in the Phillips curve. Remember, we found that price increases could increase output in the short run. By our reasoning, this was because the price increase enabled businessmen to increase nominal wages while still allowing real wages to fall. Because the inflation was unex-

---

[1] SOURCE: *Economic Report of the President*, (Washington, D. C., 1971).

pected, this situation induced higher than equilibrium labor supply and labor demand, a happy but temporary state of affairs. This is exactly what the Phillips curve says: wage increases reduce unemployment. But if the output-inflation trade-off was short run, temporary, so should the Phillips curve trade-off between wage boosts and unemployment be short run. They are merely different views of the same process.

Is there a long-run Phillips curve, and if so, what does it look like? Such a curve would tell us the relation between long-run equilibrium unemployment and wage changes, when there is no unexpected inflation. When inflation is fully forecast, no price change by itself can increase employment, because the change is immediately offset by an equal increase in nominal wages. In the long run the only possible equilibrium in the labor market is the intersection of labor demand and labor supply curves. This determines employment and the real wage. At that real wage a certain additional number of people are seeking work. These are the long-run equilibrium unemployed; the number of such unemployed constitutes what has been termed the natural rate of employment.

Wage increases by themselves would increase the number of men willing to work, but businessmen are not willing to pay the higher wages unless they are offset by price increases. But if they are offset by price increases, no additional men are willing to work. In the long run, only one level of unemployment is possible. By the term natural unemployment, we do not mean that this number is fixed and inevitable. Increasing information about job vacancies, retraining programs, and so on, would tend to lower unemployment. But at any point in time, with given labor market conditions, what we have on the Phillips curve diagram is a vertical line at the natural level of unemployment (see Figure 6.6).

Stabilization Paths

In Chapter 5 we showed how the inflationary cycle generates different paths around the long-run economy supply curve depending on whether labor expectations adjust to inflation.

102

Long-Run
Phillips Curve

Figure 6.6

Change
in wages

Natural unemployment

Unemployment

In the Phillips curve diagram, inflation generates movements around the long-run Phillips curve.

Consider first an economy where there is no adjustment of expectations. In such an economy the expansion phase of an inflation is the leftward movement up a particular short-run Phillips curve from A to B, and the stabilization phase retraces the route back down the curve to its intersection with the long-run curve (B to A) (see Figure 6.7).

When there is an adjustment of expectations in response to unexpected inflation, there are two different inflationary cycles. As the economy moves up a short-run curve, there is a gradual shift to higher and higher short-run curves. This means that one possible path is a temporary rise in employment and output counterbalanced by a permanent increase in the rate of inflation. Note that the upward-shifting curve means that the economy can reach its long-run equilibrium unemployment level with any level of inflation. In the long run, employment is not a function of price or the rate of inflation. If the government accepts an inflation of 6 percent a year, for example, and if it is fully anticipated by labor and business, the entire system adjusts to that level of inflation.

Suppose that, during a boom, an economy is moving left up the short-run Phillips curve in Figure 6.8. As prices begin to rise, labor quickly adjusts its expectations to the new inflation. In effect, the economy has shifted onto a higher short-run curve, and the economy cannot even move back to its former long-run equilibrium inflation rate without a change in expectations. If the government is willing to accept the new higher level of inflation, the path traced by the economy as it returns to the natural rate of unemployment is shown in Figure 6.8. Under this sequence the trade-off between unemployment and inflation represented by the Phillips curve becomes instead temporary supernormal employment and output followed by a permanent rise in the rate of inflation. The temporary reduction in unemployment during the expansion stage occurs when the increases in prices and wages rise above the anticipated rate. It is not the rate of inflation that produces the result; it is the *change* in the rate.

How can the rate of inflation be brought back to its original level? How can the economy return to the point A from which

Inflationary Cycle
with No Adjustment
in Expectations
Figure 6.7

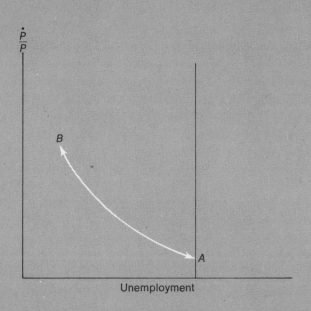

Stabilization Path
with Adjustment
in Expectations
Figure 6.8

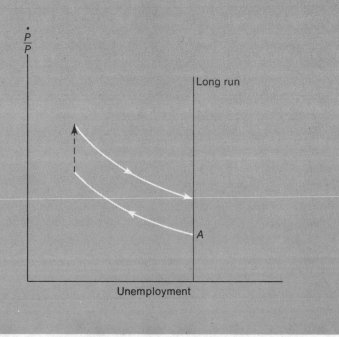

it started the inflationary cycle? According to our analysis, this requires a reduction in labor's expectations about inflation, which can probably be brought about only by a period of less than expected inflation. But when actual inflation is less than expected inflation, there is greater than normal unemployment. Hence, during the phase when expectations are being revised downward, the economy must be to the right of the long-run Phillips curve, in range B of Figure 6.9. Why? Because during the adjustment period, labor is acting on the assumption that prices will rise more than they actually do. The actual real wage rises above its long-run equilibrium level, and this rise increases unemployment. In other words, the economy moves out on curve 2 to the right of the vertical line in Figure 6.9. Gradually, as actual inflation remains below expected, forecasts adapt and the economy moves back down to curve 1, as shown by the dotted lines in the figure.

The economy comes full circle, returning to its initial position. But the cost of the boom period is not just a temporary increase in the rate of inflation. With positive expected inflation, it is not possible to take a one-way trip to the left of the long-run natural rate of unemployment. The economy is forced to endure a stabilization period of more than normal unemployment while expectations fall back to the original level. The cost of the temporary reduction in unemployment is a later period of greater than normal unemployment. So the choice facing the economy, the trade-off if you will, is not employment versus inflation; rather it is employment now or later, output now or later.

In the United States, the cost of the boom years 1965–1969, when the unemployment rate dropped to less than 4 percent, is the current stabilization period, when the unemployment rate must remain at above 4 percent in order that the economy can return to the 1 to 2 percent rate of inflation it had before the boom began. The longer it takes people to adjust downward their expectations to lower rates of inflation, the longer must be the period of more than normal unemployment. As this is written (February 1971) the adjustment appears to be quite slow. If the adjustment continues at this slow pace, the unexpected inflation of the late 1960s will be a very costly

A Complete Inflationary Cycle with Adjustment in Expectations

Figure 6.9

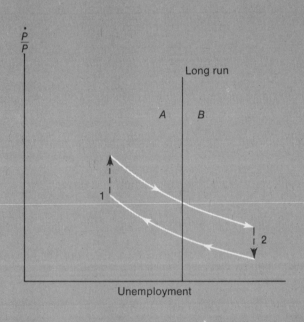

way of achieving a temporary increase in output and employment.

In the long run, the surest way to increase the number of men working and the amount of output they produce is to increase the productivity of the labor force. The surest way to reduce the natural rate of unemployment is to eliminate the reasons for it. These reasons are, primarily, the workers' uncertainty about alternative job opportunities and their inability to retrain for new jobs. A greater flow of information about job vacancies, lists of going wage rates being paid, and vigorous programs of retraining are all helpful. In the long run there is no cheap way of increasing a country's production or employment. Inflation seems to offer an answer, but that is illusory. At *best* the extra output is temporary. It is much more likely to be offset by less than normal output and employment sometime in the future.

Questions

1. How might the Phillips curve traced by an economy in which there is a fast adjustment of expectations to inflation differ from the curve traced by an economy with slowly adopting expectations?
2. If, in the long run, there is no trade-off between inflation and unemployment, then in order to reduce the long-run unemployment level we would want to undertake policies designed to shift the long-run Phillips curve to the left. What policies would you suggest for accomplishing this goal?
3. Attempt to derive a Phillips curve, using the aggregate demand-aggregate supply analysis of the previous chapters.
4. "If, in the past, the government had used the Phillips curve relation as a guide to policy formulation, we would never have observed such a relation." What does this statement mean?
5. Explain what was meant by the phrase "inflation on the installment plan."

6. How would you explain to your mother that it is possible to have rising inflation and rising unemployment at the same time? (Is it possible?)

Suggestions for Further Reading

Hansen, Bent, "Excess Demand, Unemployment, Vacancies and Wages," *Quarterly Journal of Economics* (February 1970), 1–24.

Holt, Charles C., and Martin H. David, "The Concept of Job Vacancies in a Dynamic Theory of the Labor Market," in *The Measurement and Interpretation of Job Vacancies*: NBER Conference Report. (New York, 1966).

Lipsey, Richard, "The Relation Between Unemployment and the Rate of Change of Money Wage Rates in the United Kingdom, 1862–1957: A Further Analysis," *Economica* (February 1960), 1–31.

Perry, George, *Unemployment, Money Wage Rates and Inflation.* Cambridge, Mass.; MIT Press, 1966.

Phelps, Edmund S., *et al.*, eds., *Microeconomic Foundations of Employment and Inflation Theory.* New York, 1970. (Especially papers by Phelps, Holt, Lucas, and Rapping and Mortenson).

Phillips, A. W., "The Relation Between Unemployment and the Rate of Change of Money Wage Rates in the United Kingdom, 1862–1957," *Economica* (November 1958), 283–299.

7
CHAPTER

Inflation and
the Distribution
of Income

During the inflationary process, prices, wages, and interest rates are all rising. In this panorama of movement in relative and absolute prices, are there systematic changes that have a predictable effect on the distribution of income? That is, is inflation like the progressive tax, redistributing income from the wealthy to the poor, or does it increase the inequality of income? Does inflation increase labor's return in relation to profits or vice versa? These are the questions this chapter investigates.

Effect of Inflation on Income of the Poor

For the poor the two principal sources of income are salaries and transfer payments. All the evidence suggests that, as a group, the poor gain during an inflation, provided it is accompanied by full employment. The reason for this advantage is that the working poor, who are usually the least skilled members of the labor force, find jobs more easily in tight labor markets. Wives of poor families enter the labor force during

Indexes of Various Forms of Public Assistance and Per Capita Disposable Income

Figure 7.1

1. Per capita disposable income (1958 dollars)
2. Aid to families with dependent children—average monthly payment
3. Unemployment insurance, state summary—average monthly for total unemployed
4. Old-age assistance per recipient—average monthly payment
5. General assistance per recipient

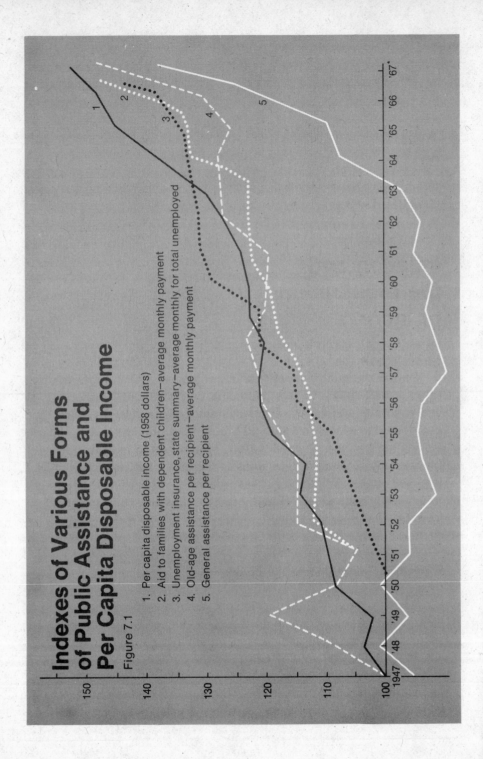

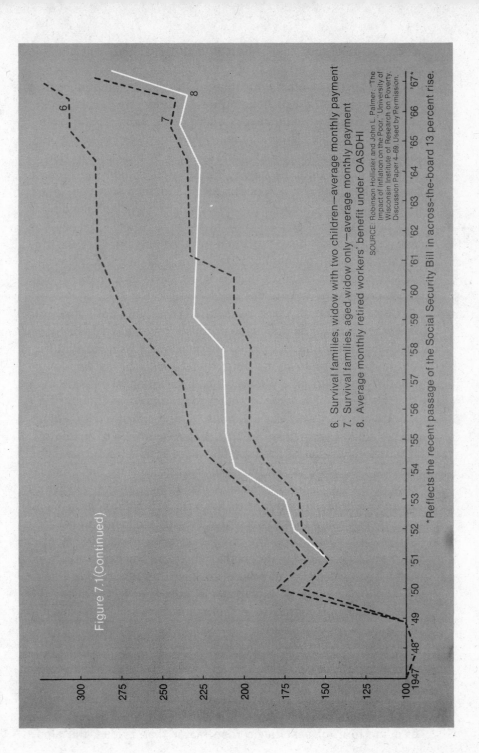

Figure 7.1(Continued)

6. Survival families, widow with two children—average monthly payment
7. Survival families, aged widow only—average monthly payment
8. Average monthly retired workers' benefit under OASDHI

SOURCE: Robinson Hollister and John L. Palmer, "The Impact of Inflation on the Poor," University of Wisconsin Institute of Research on Poverty, Discussion Paper 4-69. Used by Permission.

*Reflects the recent passage of the Social Security Bill in across-the-board 13 percent rise.

113

such periods and find jobs. In addition, wage differentials narrow.

If changes in employment associated with inflation cause the favorable effect of inflation on the poor, we would expect that the relation would reverse during the stabilization phase. During the expansionary phase, labor markets are tight. Employment increases, causing the income of the poor to rise in relation to the national mean. During stabilization the reverse occurs. Tight labor markets disappear and unemployment rises, even though inflation may continue unabated. In these conditions the poor suffer. Because they depend so heavily on salaries and wages, they bear the brunt of stabilization, just as they gain most from economic expansion. Thus the income distribution tends to equalize during boom periods and to become more unequal during recessions.

Booms generally are associated with inflation, and this is what makes inflation appear to be favorable to the poor. But, as we have seen, inflation is consistent with many different levels of employment. Thus there should be no one-to-one relation between inflation and the distribution of income.

The other main income source of the poor is transfer payments, such as welfare, pensions, and social security. Rising prices could harm this group, relatively or even absolutely, if the money value of the transfers they receive is not adjusted upward. A recent study has shown that during the postwar period welfare, social security, and other transfer payments actually increased faster than the rate of inflation. This alone would not ensure that the recipients were not losing in relation to the rest of the population. If real growth occurs, income earners will also be increasing their incomes, so that adjustments in welfare payments to keep the purchasing power of these payments constant would still lead to a fall in the share of income going to welfare and pension recipients. In a period of growth it is not enough to keep constant the size of the piece of the pie going to persons on welfare, pensions, and social security. When the size of the pie increases, the piece going to this group must also increase.

In Figure 7.1 we show the deflated value of different forms of per capita monthly payments. Whenever the nominal value of some form of assistance rose faster than prices, the slope of this line on the graph is positive. It can be seen at a glance that transfer payments have been increasing in real terms almost continuously in the postwar period.

How have transfers fared in relation to disposable income? To get the answer graphically, compare the slopes of the disposable income and transfer lines on the diagram. If the disposable income line rises more rapidly than that of transfers, the income distribution is moving against transfer recipients. A comparison of the various lines on the graph suggests that disposable income and transfer payments have by and large

TABLE 7.1

Share of Money Income Before Taxes of Certain Percentiles of Population[1]

	25%	35%	Top 10%	Unemployment Rate
1948	5.4	10.8	28.9	3.8
1949	5.2	10.4	28.7	5.9
1950	5.0	10.2	28.9	5.3
1951	5.4	10.9	27.9	3.3
1952	5.5	11.0	27.9	3.0
1954	4.9	10.0	28.2	5.5
1955	5.1	10.4	27.7	4.4
1956	5.3	10.7	27.4	4.1
1957	4.9	10.0	27.0	4.3
1958	5.2	10.6	27.1	6.8
1959	5.1	10.4	27.7	5.5
1960	5.1	10.4	27.9	5.5
1961	5.0	10.1	28.7	6.7
1962	5.3	10.5	27.5	5.5
1963	5.3	10.5	27.3	5.7
1964	5.3	10.5	27.4	5.2
1965	5.5	10.7	27.5	4.5
1966	5.6	10.9	27.3	3.8
1967	5.7	10.9	27.7	3.8
1968	5.9	11.3	27.1	3.6

[1] SOURCE: Edward C. Budd, "Postwar Changes in the Size Distribution of Income in the U. S.," American Economic Review (May 1970).

grown together during the postwar period. Transfers were adjusted to reflect not only inflation but also changes in the level of real income. Thus the expectation that inflation might hurt the poor who live on pensions, welfare, and other transfers is not borne out by the record.

With this introduction we now turn to measures of the distribution of income during the postwar period. We could use many different measures to investigate the changing share of money income received by different groups of the population. If we order people by the size of their incomes, we can look at the share of total income received by the bottom 25 percent or 35 percent to see how the poor have fared in relation to the whole population, and we can look at the share of the top 10 percent to get the same indicator for the rich. Greater equality is represented by a fall in the share of the upper group and by a rise in the share of the lower group.

In the lower income group, the relation between unemployment levels and the percentage of total income received is quite marked. When the unemployment rate dropped below 4 percent, as it did during the Korean War and after 1965, the income share rose above 5.4 percent. During stabilization periods such as 1949, 1954, and 1957–1960 the share dropped to around 5 percent. For the upper income group the relation is less clear. The expansion in the 1960s was marked by a steady decline in relative position, as was the period of Korea. Stabilization was beneficial—observe 1954 or the period 1957–1960.[2]

Crude as our measure is, it confirms the cyclic pattern of the size distribution of income we expected to find. Periods of tight labor markets are beneficial to the poor, while high unemployment quickly reduces their relative position. Stabilization is beneficial, and expansion harmful to this group, in relative terms.

What is the relation of all this to inflation? We have said

[2] For further evidence supporting the cyclic movement of the size distribution of income, see Charles E. Metcalf, "The Size Distribution of Personal Income during the Business Cycle," *American Economic Review* (September 1969), and Lester C. Thurow, "Analyzing the American Income Distribution," *American Economic Review* (May 1970).

that the really important determinant of income distribution behavior over the business cycle is the tightness of the labor market, which we can represent by the amount of unemployment. Now if there is a dependable relation between unemployment and the rate of inflation, we would expect an equally dependable relation between inflation and the size distribution of income. That is, if the Phillips curve represents alternative steady states, we should expect inflation to benefit the poor. If there is a trade-off between inflation and unemployment, the higher the inflation the lower the unemployment, and therefore the higher the income share of the poor.

We have argued, however, that the Phillips curve does not represent a trade-off. In the long run, the only viable unemployment rate is the natural rate. If we are right, the income gains of the poor during the cyclic move up the Phillips curve are temporary. These gains will be taken away when the economy moves back to the long-run employment level. When the economy moves from *A* to *B* in Figure 7.2, the poor gain. If the economy could stay at *B*, this gain would be permanent. But this depends on the public's never expecting inflation. If the public does expect inflation, the Phillips curve begins to drift upward. To return to point *A* now requires a period of stabilization, of supernormal unemployment, while expectations are brought back to their original level. This is the opposite of the original gains made from tight labor markets. Now the poor not only give up all the gains received in moving from point *A* to point *B*, but also fall below their long-run income share because of supernormal unemployment during stabilization.

Many have claimed that inflation hurts the poor because of their dependence on welfare payments and pensions. This claim proves to be wrong. We can say, however, that inflation hurts the poor in one special sense. Although the employment gains characteristic of the expansion phase of an inflation benfit the poor, they are temporary. We have not found a way to hold the economy at less than normal unemployment levels without an acceleration of inflation. An economic policy implying accelerating inflation has never been accepted. The expansion phase of an inflation is therefore doomed to be followed by a stabilization phase. During that phase all the

Changes in Income Shares and the Phillips Curve

Figure 7.2

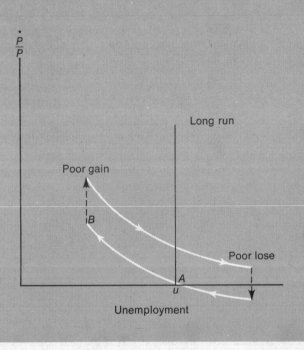

previous gains of the poor are wiped out. The inequality of the income distribution is heightened. So, for the poor, the gains in the one period must be weighed against the losses in the succeeding period. Unfortunately we seem to be quite inefficient at stabilization. It takes a long time. Thus the gains to the poor during expansion may be enjoyed for far fewer years than the erosion during stabilization.

We can illustrate this point by referring to the 1950s. During the Korean War there was a three-year period of super-normal employment, rising prices, and an income distribution favorable to the poor. But this period was followed by a six-year period of intermittent stabilization during which the inflation was finally contained. All the previous gains of the poor were wiped out. Looking at it from the perspective of the entire cycle, the Korean inflation was not advantageous to the poor. We could conclude that, *given our inefficiency in stabilizing*, inflation is costly to the poor.

Inflation and the Uses of Income

We have concentrated so far on the effect of inflation on earnings. It is also possible that inflation could affect differently the real spending power of different groups. That is, the prices of the things the poor buy could rise by less or more than the prices of those bought by the rich. In that case the inflation would change the distribution of real purchasing power even if it did not affect the distribution of nominal income. A recent study, investigating possible differential impacts of inflation on spending power, constructed a poor man's cost of living index.[3] This index rises by slightly less than the average consumer price index during inflations. This is especially true if the aged poor, with their high expenditures on medical care, are removed from the poor population. Thus on the spending side there is no evidence that inflation discriminates against the poor.

---

[3] Robinson G. Hollister and John L. Palmer, "The Impact of Inflation on the Poor," University of Wisconsin, Institute for Research on Poverty, Discussion Paper, 40–69.

Inflation and Wealth

Aside from its effect on income, inflation has important effects on the real value of wealth and its distribution. The prices of real assets such as land or houses tend to rise during inflations, thus protecting their owners against a potential loss of purchasing power. Fixed-value assets such as bonds, bank deposits, or life insurance policies all fall in real terms.

In order to quantify the effect of inflation on the distribution of real wealth, one must first construct an inventory of assets by income class, then try to estimate the likely price reaction of each asset to inflation. One recent study has attempted to do this, and we summarize its results.[4]

The poor are, by and large, debtors. Debtors, we know, generally benefit from an inflation, because the real cost of repaying loans falls. This should be especially true during the expansion phase of an inflation, when lenders are caught unawares by rising prices. When lenders raise the nominal interest rate they charge to offset the rise in prices over the life of the loan, this inflationary redistribution of real purchasing power from the creditor to the debtor should disappear.

As we proceed up the income distribution, the asset-debt ratio rises. This rise would lead us to expect that inflation tends to equalize the distribution of real wealth; that is, inflation should act like a tax on the wealthy, which is exactly what Budd found in his recent study. Once again, this is during the initial phase before asset holders have learned to adjust nominal interest rates for inflation.

One might ask, what about common stocks? It used to be an adage on Wall Street that when one expected inflation, he invested in common stocks. Corporate earnings should rise with inflation, and so therefore should stock prices. Since ownership of common stocks is concentrated in the upper income groups, this could offset the equalizing effect of inflation on real wealth. Note two points in this regard. First, and most important, there is no necessary relation between stock prices and inflation, as speculators found to their sorrow

---

[4] Edward C. Budd and David F. Seiders, "The Impact of Inflation on the Distribution of Income and Wealth," *American Economic Review* (May 1971).

in the years 1969–1970. Second, Budd, in the study just referred to, did assume that stock prices rose faster than prices. Even at that, the wealthy lost in relation to the poor.

Is it obvious that stock prices must rise in inflations? As so often before, we must distinguish between the expansionary phase and the stabilization phase. During expansion, profits rise and wealth holders switch from fixed-value assets such as bonds to stocks. Stock prices rise. During stabilizations it is a different matter. Corporate earnings fall and the decreases reduce stock prices. In addition, the government in its attempt to stabilize typically uses monetary policy. It sells bonds, and this drives bond prices down and interest rates up. Bonds and stocks are substitute ways of holding wealth. When bond rates rise, the increase makes bonds attractive in relation to stocks. Prices of stocks fall as the public switches into higher yielding bonds. As one can see by the record, periods of tight money and high interest rates tend to bring recessions on Wall Street. The shaded areas in Figure 7.3 are periods of restrictive monetary policy, all of which were associated with declines in stock prices.

What has all this to do with inflation? To the extent that stabilizations are linked to, or brought about because of, previous periods of inflationary expansion, we cannot look at the gains of the former without including the later losses. The full effect of inflation on stock prices would have to include both the gains of the expansionary period *and* the losses during stabilization. This is exactly the same as our discussion of the effect of inflation on unemployment. Because Budd's study does not recognize the negative impact of stabilization on stock prices, it may well be biased upward. The actual effect of inflation on wealth may be even more equalizing than Budd estimates. We are probably safe in concluding that inflation is like a progressive tax on the assets of the rich.

Inflation, Factor Returns, and the Functional Distribution of Income

We have been investigating the effect of inflation on the size distribution of income—on the share of the pie going to different income classes. An equally important question is

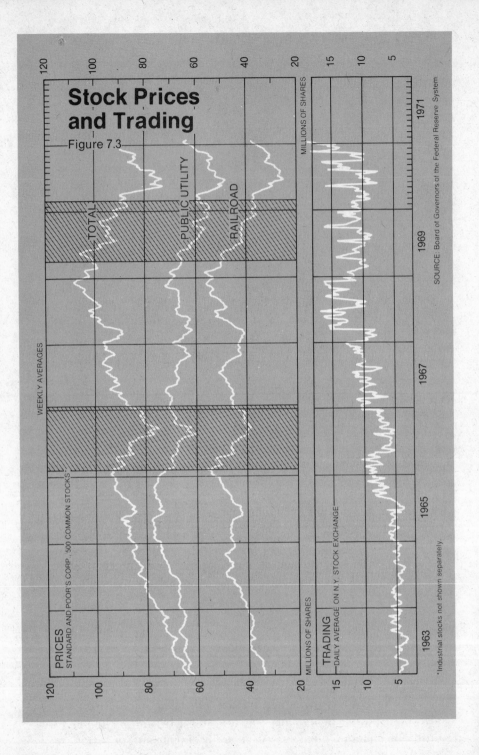

Stock Prices and Trading

Figure 7.3

PRICES
STANDARD AND POOR'S CORP. 500 COMMON STOCKS

WEEKLY AVERAGES

TOTAL

PUBLIC UTILITY

RAILROAD

MILLIONS OF SHARES

TRADING
DAILY AVERAGE ON N.Y. STOCK EXCHANGE

MILLIONS OF SHARES

1963   1965   1967   1969   1971

120   100   80   60   40   20

15   10   5

*Industrial stocks not shown separately.

SOURCE: Board of Governors of the Federal Reserve System

122

how inflation influences the division of the pie between the factors of production—workers and capitalists. Our theory makes definite predictions about the behavior of factor shares during the two stages of inflation. It predicts that during the expansionary phase, rising prices and productivity lower the real cost of labor and enable business to increase employment. During stabilizations, wage demands exceed the rise in prices and productivity. Labor costs rise and employment falls. Let us see how these predictions have been borne out in recent years.

In Table 7.2 observe the behavior of two series, real wages and wages per dollar of sales. The real wage, as we know, represents the amount of output the worker gets in exchange for an hour of labor. The second measure, which we have not used before, is the labor cost per dollar of sales. It compares the change in labor productivity with the change in the real wage. According to our model, business should hire more workers whenever this ratio falls. Why? Because the fall represents a drop in the cost of labor to the firm. For constant labor productivity per hour, a fall in the ratio is a decline in real wages; whereas for rising productivity, a decline means that real wages rose less than productivity.

During the early part of an expansion the demand for labor is increasing, because of rising productivity. Since unemployment is high, small increases in nominal wages are sufficient to increase employment. Thus we find a simultaneous increase in the real wage and a fall in labor costs per dollar of sales. In the United States this stage lasted through 1965. Unemployment fell from 5.5 percent to 4.5 percent, annual inflation was less than 2 percent, and real wages were increasing.

From 1966 onward, the economy entered a period of more rapid inflation. No doubt labor was beginning to make adjustments in its expectations. Yet employment continued to rise, because, despite the rise in real wages, the real cost of labor continued to fall.

During the stabilization period which began in 1969 the situation was reversed. Labor demanded catch-up wage boosts large enough to reverse the downward movement in real labor costs. The result was a predictable fall in employment.

So much for factor prices. What do our results imply about factor shares during the inflationary process? To go from

123

TABLE 7.2

Labor Cost[5]

Year	Real Wage* 1967 = 100	Index of Wages/Sales† 1967 = 100
1950	72.0	137.1
1951	72.0	129.0
1952	74.1	129.5
1953	77.5	129.0
1954	79.6	134.2
1955	82.4	128.1
1956	85.5	130.3
1957	86.8	130.5
1958	88.0	134.1
1959	90.0	128.2
1960	91.5	127.3
1961	93.3	127.5
1962	94.6	121.0
1963	95.7	117.4
1964	96.9	112.4
1965	97.8	106.5
1966	98.3	100.6
1967	100.0	100.0
1968	101.8	97.0
1969	102.3	94.8
1970	103.5	96.3

* Index of average hourly earnings in manufacturing deflated by CPI.
† Real wage divided by index of output per man-hour.

factor shares is more of a jump than it might seem at first glance. While we can predict what happens to wages and profits, we would need to know percentage changes in each to predict whether the laborer's or the capitalist's slice of the national income pie increased. To do this would require empirical knowledge about shapes of supply and demand curves, which we do not have. In other words, our theory cannot predict the behavior of factor shares during an inflation without additional information. Thus we must be content with description.

---

[5] SOURCE: *Economic Report of the President* (Washington, D. C., 1971).

Table 7.2 confirms the prediction that during the expansionary phase of an inflation the labor cost per dollar of sales should be falling. This prediction would certainly imply that business profits should be increasing in both nominal and real terms during the expansionary phase. The opposite should be true during stabilization, when labor is catching up for previous inflation and real labor costs per unit of output are rising. Both of these expectations are confirmed by the data shown in Table 7.3.

Clearly the expansion phase of an inflation benefits business. Even though the real wage of labor rises, labor's cost to business falls in real terms, a fact that is disguised by rising prices. Thus we see profits as a share of sales rising during periods of expansionary inflations, such as 1962–1968 inflation.

But the gains for business during expansions are lost during stabilization. We see this in the 1956–1960 and the 1969–1970 periods. It is just what we would expect. During the stabilization period aggregate demand falls in real terms, generally because the government is trying to stabilize. But labor, now aware of previous inflation, continues to raise its wage demands so that the labor costs per unit of output often rise. Thus, like all the other groups we have studied, business and labor gain during one phase of an inflation and lose during another.

One group appears to gain uniformly from all inflations— government. In Chapter 4 we showed how inflation increases tax receipts in real terms because of the progressivity of the tax system. Thus the government share tends to rise whenever prices do, and this rise occurs in both phases of the inflationary process.

When we review our discussion of the effect of inflation on both the size and the functional distribution of income, the recurrent theme which stands out is that no group gains uniformly throughout an inflation. Groups, like the poor or business, that gain the most during expansions lose the most during stabilization. Those which lose ground in relation to the population during expansions, such as the wealthy or labor, tend to recoup those losses during the succeeding stabilization. Thus, to paraphrase, in an inflation there seem to be no winners or no losers, only survivors.

TABLE 7.3
Measures of Profitability[6]

	Corporate Profits (before taxes) * (in billions of 1967 dollars)	Profits† Sales
1950	$52.3	12.8%
1951	54.9	11.2
1952	50.2	9.2
1953	49.4	9.2
1954	47.2	8.4
1955	58.5	10.3
1956	56.6	9.7
1957	54.1	8.8
1958	47.5	7.4
1959	59.2	8.8
1960	56.3	8.0
1961	56.1	7.7
1962	61.5	8.2
1963	64.2	8.5
1964	71.4	8.9
1965	80.5	9.4
1966	84.8	9.3
1967	78.7	8.3
1968	82.0	8.8
1969	78.1	8.4
1970	67.1§	6.6‡

* All industries. † All manufacturing corporations.
‡ Third quarter. § Profit is average of first three quarters.

The reason for our conclusion is the connection between different parts of the inflationary cycle or process. Because stabilizations follow expansions, no group gains from inflation. If there was a way for an economy to have the expansion without a gradual acceleration of inflation, groups like the unemployed would gain from inflation, because a government could choose a point on a short-run Phillips curve with a low level of unemployment. Inflation would be a means of reducing

---

[6] SOURCE: *Economic Report of the President*, (Washington, D. C., 1971).

the inequality of the income distribution and of permanently helping the poor. All our theory, however, suggests that it is not possible to stay at such a low unemployment point. To do so requires that the public continue to expect one rate of inflation even when it always has a different one. When the public adjusts its expectations, the government is forced to stabilize and the inflationary benefits of the unemployed or the poor are withdrawn.

What we do not know is how fast the adjustment of expectations occurs. One would have to agree with Hollister and Palmer (see Suggestions for Further Reading) that we have spent a large part of the postwar period finding out about the relation between prices and high levels of unemployment at great cost to the poor, but we have few observations in the low unemployment range. Thus we do not really know how fast the economy drifts up from the short-run Phillips curve. We do not know how long an inflationary expansion could last before the acceleration of prices demanded a change in policy, because we have stabilized at the first signs of inflation. How many years, for example, could the United States economy have maintained the 1967 unemployment rate of 3.8 percent before the rate of inflation became unacceptable? We do not know. And this is unfortunate; because if the reaction to inflation were slow, then this kind of cautious reduction in unemployment might well be a viable way of permanently reducing poverty in the United States.

Questions

1. Why would we expect the government's share of real GNP to increase during both stages of the inflation? Under what conditions would the government's share not increase? Would it ever decrease?
2. We have indicated in this chapter that many groups which are harmed (helped) during the expansion stage of the inflation are helped (harmed) during the stabilization phase. If the real income losses are eventually more or less

balanced by real income gains, why should policy makers be concerned about inflation?

3. During the expansion phase of an inflation unemployment falls. Is the reduction in unemployment necessarily beneficial or efficient?

4. Why can't our theory predict what happens to factor shares during an inflation? What additional information would be necessary in order to make such predictions?

5. Following the theory we have developed, describe how income is likely to be redistributed among the various income and factor groups over the entire inflationary process.

Suggestions for Further Reading

Bach, George L., and Albert Ando, "The Redistributional Effects of Inflation," *Review of Economics and Statistics* (February 1957), 1–13.

Burger, Albert E., "The Effects of Inflation (1960–1968)," *Federal Reserve Bank of St. Louis Review* (November 1969).

Felix, David, "Profit Inflation and Industrial Growth: The Historic Record and Contemporary Analogies," *Quarterly Journal of Economics* (August 1956), 441–463.

Hollister, Robinson, and John L. Palmer, "The Impact of Inflation on the Poor," Institute for Research on Poverty Discussion Paper #40–69.

Kessel, R. A., "Inflation-Caused Wealth Redistribution: A Hypothesis," *American Economic Review* (March 1956), 128–241.

Metcalf, Charles E., "The Size Distribution of Personal Income During the Business Cycle," *American Economic Review* (September 1969), 657–667.

Pesek, Boris P., "Distribution Effects of Inflation and Taxation," *American Economic Review* (March 1960), 147–153.

8
CHAPTER

The
Problem
of Stabilization

Stabilizing an economy after a period of inflation is probably the most delicate and difficult economic maneuver that a government can attempt. Stabilization at such a time means inevitably a cutting back in some direction—someone's spending and consumption must fall; someone must lose his job. It is the morning after an economic blast. Are there better and worse ways to get through this unpleasant morning-after? The goal of stabilization is to return to a desired rate of increase in prices, with the least possible loss in production during the transition period. In deciding on the target rate of inflation, the authorities have to balance the cost of stabilization against the cost of inflation. We already know that the cost of stabilization is a period of dislocation, falling output, and high unemployment. What are the costs of inflation? Why not simply accept whatever rate is being forecast by labor and adjust the entire system to it?

One cost of inflation is that it causes the economic system to operate inefficiently. In Chapter 2 we showed how inflation induces people to reduce their money holdings and to change their saving behavior in ways that make less productive capital available to the economy. People devote time, and business devotes labor, to avert inflationary redistributions of real wealth. Such action is inefficient. Moreover, inflation is discriminatory. Unless inflation is perfectly anticipated, it can cause rather dramatic changes in real income shares in the short run. These attributes are undesirable.

The government has to balance the inefficiencies and inequities introduced by an inflation against the temporary costs of reducing the inflation to some desired level. Quite clearly, the longer the inflation continues, the longer will be the period of adjustment to a lower actual rate. The reason is because the public, and especially labor, will have become accustomed to that historic rate of inflation. They will be expecting it to continue in the future, and it will take some time before their expectations adjust to the lower rate. During the adjustment period the levels of output and employment are undoubtedly going to be less than normal, because actual real wages rise above their long-run equilibrium levels.

Once again we should stress the fundamental difference between stabilization with zero and positive expected inflation. When labor expects no future change in prices, wages need rise only enough to offset previous inflation. There is a one-time further increase in prices, an elimination of involuntary unemployment, and the process ends. There is no period of more than normal unemployment, no period of excess capacity. Stabilization involves nothing more than giving up more than normal output levels.

When inflation is expected in the future, nominal wages rise by enough to offset it. Now the government, in its attempt to stabilize, must produce a rate of actual inflation lower than what is expected, in order to reduce these expectations. When it does that, the actual real wage rises above its equilibrium level, meaning that unemployment rises above its long-run normal rate. Thus, if an inflation has gone on long enough so that expected inflation is positive, the public must expect stabilization to lead to a period of greater than normal unemployment, excess capacity, and unused resources while the economy adjusts to the lower rate. The longer the inflation, the higher the likely unemployment during stabilization.

Our analysis implies that the cost and the difficulty of stabilizing vary directly with the length of the preceding inflation. There must be cases where the history of inflation is so long that stabilization per se is not an optimal policy. That is, the cost of continuing the inflation may well be less than the cost of stabilizing. It may then be wiser to adapt the economy to the inflation by introducing automatic escalators in all wage and mortgage contracts than to try to eliminate the inflation through an extended period of unemployment. Price stability is not an end in itself. It is just one characteristic of an economy whose benefits may or may not be worth the cost of achievement.

Gradual versus Rapid Stabilization

Given that a government has decided to stabilize, should the program be fast or slow? The more the government restricts demand, the faster the inflation will disappear, but the higher will be the temporary unemployment. If the gradual route is chosen, the interim unemployment level will be lower, but it will take longer to reach the desired rate of inflation. One way to compare alternatives is to compare the total number of man-years of employment and output lost through supernormal unemployment during stabilization.

The choice is dependent on how fast people adjust to lower than anticipated rates of inflation. Suppose, for example, that labor's expected rate of inflation is just equal to the actual rate during the previous period. This would be very rapid adjustment. The government could eliminate expected inflation by forcing price stability during only one period. Of course, such action might involve a very high one-period unemployment level, but it might be a politically feasible level, because it would quickly bring price stability.

When price expectations change slowly, even high rates of unemployment will only gradually reduce the inflation, and these high rates are likely to be much harder to sell politically. Remember that the cost of gradualness is a longer period of subnormal employment and more inflation. In other words, a slower approach to price stability does not necessarily mean that the total number of unemployed man-years is fewer, but the number is spread over a longer time span. Most governments opt for gradual stabilization, one suspects, not because total unemployment is less, but because the high levels of a rapid program are more costly politically. The public discounts the future and prefers higher employment today, even if this means higher unemployment tomorrow. Suppose, for example, that an economy has a normal rate of unemployment of 4 percent and that it has two alternative paths to price stability: 7 percent unemployment for two years and 4 percent thereafter, or 5 percent for six years and 4 percent thereafter. In both paths the same total number of man-years is lost through supernormal unemployment, namely 6 percent of the labor force. Yet the 5 percent rate would probably be preferable to the 7 percent rate, even though unemployment would have to last for six years and would mean permanently higher prices.

Monetary versus Fiscal Policy

Once a stabilization path and a time profile are agreed upon, the orthodox government has two principal tools for controlling aggregate demand, monetary policy and fiscal policy. It can raise taxes, reduce its expenditures, or limit the expansion of the money supply by selling government bonds and/or raising reserve requirements. Neither set of policies is without problems.

Fiscal policy as practiced in the United States has been limited to some control over government spending and temporary increases in the personal income tax. It has proved to be extremely difficult to make significant reductions in government spending, partly because of the large military budget, but also partly because the other programs are by and large important to different segments of the population and are defended vigorously by them. During 1968, while the government was most actively trying to control inflation, we find that the government purchase of goods and services expanded not only in nominal terms but also in real terms. Most of the expansion occurred in state and local governments, but the point is that government functions, like private ones, are difficult to defer in response to a stabilization program.

If the government finds it difficult to cut its own budgets, it has the alternative of raising taxes to force the private sector to reduce consumption and investment. Economic theory maintains that consumption is a function of disposable income, so that if personal income taxes are increased, the share of consumption in GNP should fall, thus reducing aggregate demand. Anti-inflationary surtaxes have, in practice, turned out to be an inflexible tool, because of the length of time it takes to sell so distasteful a remedy. Take as an example the 10 percent surtax imposed in 1968 on corporate and personal incomes in the United States. It was proposed by President Lyndon B. Johnson in his budget message in January 1967. Despite the mounting evidence of inflationary pressure in the economy, the bill was not signed until June 1968. Even though the tax was retroactive to January 1968 for corporations and April for individuals, the delay was long and costly. And this is only the first of the lags between the need for the tax and its final effect on spending. Experience with the same surtax has shown us that there is much delay before private consumption begins to fall. Study the figures shown in Table 8.1.

TABLE 8.1

Ratio of Disposable Income to GNP and of Consumption to GNP

Year	Disposable Income / GNP	Consumption / Disposable Income	Consumption / GNP
1966	68.3%	93.6%	62.2%
1967	68.9	92.3	62.0
1968	68.2	93.5	62.0
1968 1st quarter	68.8	93.1	62.3
2d quarter	68.4	92.8	61.8
3d quarter	67.7	94.4	62.2 (surtax)
4th quarter	67.7	93.7	61.7
1969	67.5	94.0	61.8
1969 1st quarter	67.2	94.7	61.8
2d quarter	67.3	94.7	61.9
3d quarter	67.8	93.3	61.4
4th quarter	67.9	93.6	61.8

During the last quarters of 1968 and the first quarters of 1969, the public reacted to the surtax by reducing saving, not consumption—for a good reason. The tax was announced as temporary. Households had the choice of reducing purchases during the period of the tax by the full amount of the tax or spreading that reduction over a number of years by reducing both consumption and saving. Because savings provide for consumption in future years, by reducing savings households were, in effect, spreading the reduced consumption over a number of years, which is surely a rational thing to do. Eventually, as the surtax was extended for a full year to June 1970, private consumption did fall, a major factor in the downturn in economic activity that began in the fourth quarter of 1969. But the lag between the first presentation of the tax surcharge and its effect spread over two years. During that time the consumer price index rose by 11 percent. A policy that is so slow is not a very effective stabilization tool.

What about monetary policy? Given the speed with which changes in the money supply can be realized, monetary policy should not suffer from the lag problem that fiscal policy does. But this is really not true. For the lag occurs between the time the money supply is reduced and the spending finally drops. This lag appears to be quite long. We generally think that restrictive monetary policy reduces investment by raising interest rates. Yet investment projects are not start-stop propositions that can be turned off when interest rates change. Even if new projects are deferred when interest rates rise, there may be no measurable effect for three to six months if that is the ordinary planning period for a project. Moreover, because interest is a taxable cost, the effect of changes in interest rates on after-tax profits is reduced by 50 percent.

Once again, consider the United States experience. To a significant extent we have relied on a policy of tight money since the beginning of 1969. During the eight months from July 1969 through February 1970, the money supply rose by less than 0.5 percent, which meant a decline of 3 percent in real terms. Nor was it much more expansive in the previous six months. Interest rates, as we know, soared to their highest levels in over one hundred years. (There is some question whether interest rates increased *real* terms during this period.)

Yet investment did not drop. Quite the contrary, during 1969 investment was one of the leading sectors in the economy, with a 10 percent increase over 1968. Only in 1970 did we finally witness the expected decline.

Beside the unavoidable lag, two other characteristics of a restrictive monetary policy are undesirable. Such a policy may have a perverse, inflationary effect on supply. After all, interest rates are a cost, the cost of capital and inventory. If tight money raises interest rates, it raises the cost of production. This can mean either lower output or higher prices, or both. Take two examples. Consider the farmer. He wants to buy fertilizer to increase his output. Suppose that tight money makes it impossible to borrow for that purpose; he therefore does not apply the fertilizer and his output falls. Total output or effective capacity in the economy falls. Of course, his demand for fertilizer falls too, and this decrease in demand is anti-inflationary, because it reduces aggregate demand. This situation produces two opposite effects—one reducing supply, the other reducing demand. Which is greater? We know that the farmer would not apply fertilizer unless the extra output it produced was worth more than it cost. We therefore know that the value of the reduction in supply exceeds the value of the reduction in demand. High interest rates can perversely increase excess demand.

All goods produced with large quantities of fixed capital become more expensive when interest rates rise, because interest measures the cost of capital. Two important components of the consumer price index, utilities and housing, are obvious examples of capital intensive goods. In recent months these have been leading factors in the inflation of the CPI, because of the rise in interest rates. Here tight money has a direct inflationary impact on the cost of living. By artificially making capital more expensive, the government is limiting the effective capacity of the economy.

The other disagreeable element in monetary policy is that it falls unequally on different sectors. When the Federal Reserve sells bonds, it reduces the funds available for private borrowers and raises the interest rate. If financial markets were perfectly interconnected, all borrowers would find funds slightly more expensive, and the burden of the policy would be equitably distributed. But our financial markets are not perfectly interconnected. A restrictive monetary policy may therefore have a far greater impact on some borrowers than on others. Rising interest rates generally have caused the public to shift their savings from financial intermediaries, such as banks and savings and loan associations, directly into the bond market. For borrowers with access to the bond market this does not cause an insurmountable problem, because they too can switch their borrowing to the bond market. But small borrowers do not have access to the bond market. Therefore, as the flow of funds through financial intermediaries is reduced during periods of high interest rates, the borrowing of the small borrower is particularly curtailed.

The most obvious example of the difficulty of small borrowers can be seen in the housing market. For institutional reasons funds for the housing market have primarily been supplied by banks and savings and loan associations. These institutions have a ceiling on the rate of interest they are permitted to pay for funds. When tight money or inflation pushes the rate of interest above that limit, borrowable funds no longer flow into this market. The result is that private-house buyers and builders are unable to find financing for their purchases. Interestingly enough a partial way around this institutional impasse has been found. Banks form holding companies, and holding companies are allowed to issue stock. In effect these companies are borrowing funds in different markets where they can pay the going rate of interest. Another attempt to meet the market imperfections in the mortgage market is the formation of the mortgage trust, a company that sells stock and then lends the money to builders. Again, the effect is to switch housing finance out of its traditional channels, where it is blocked by institutional restrictions.

Even with these stratagems it still seems that the burden of tight money falls heavily on the housing industry. For example, in 1969 housing investment fell by around $2 billion over the course of the year. Even granting that this decrease does reduce aggregate demand, why should builders and house buyers have to bear the brunt of the effort to control inflation?

Builders are not the only ones who suffer during prolonged periods of high interest rates. Small businesses are also hurt, because they typically depend on banks for financing. Because they cannot easily raise outside funds by floating their own promissory notes in the corporate bond market, when bank funds dry up, they should be particularly disadvantaged by periods of tight money. Many of the mergers during 1969 are said to have been caused by the inability of one of the companies to continue operations because of borrowing problems.

We seem to be left with no good way to reduce aggregate demand during stabilization. Fiscal policy and monetary policy have serious drawbacks. Is there no better tool? We think that perhaps there is. Remember that the goal of a stabilization policy is to reduce aggregate demand. Suppose that the reason for excess demand is that some new government program was unwisely financed by deficit spending. If the program is permanent, some permanent tax mechanism must be found to pay for it, ideally levied on those who will enjoy the benefits of the program. Perhaps the extra spending is temporary, in which case we would like to find some temporary tax. Temporary income taxes have a weak effect on consumption, at least initially, precisely because they are temporary. Saving, not consumption, seems to be reduced in the short run. An alternative tax, whose temporary nature would work in the right direction and not in the wrong, might be a tax on all durable purchases, both by business and by consumers. The government would announce that for a specified period all capital goods purchasers would pay a temporary sales tax. The public would thus be encouraged to delay its purchases—exactly what the government wants. Obviously such a policy would work only if the tax, and the need for it, was temporary. Such a tax puts the burden where it belongs, on those who insist on spending. Earning is not what is causing the inflation; rather it is spending. A temporary sales tax would be like a fine— discouraging behavior that is temporarily harmful to the economy.

Wage and Price Controls or Guideposts

Almost inevitably comments about the wisdom of some form of government intervention in price and wage setting arise during an inflation. The rationale for these comments is the identification of rising prices as the cause of inflation. To stop the inflation, therefore, the government need only decree the end of price increases. This confuses the symptom with the cause. As Milton Friedman has stated, it is as if the doctor attempted to cure a patient's fever by stopping the mercury in the thermometer from rising. Yet it is possible that the rise in prices in response to excess demand could be moderated by some form of price-wage guidelines or controls.

What we mean by a wage-price policy is some intervention by the government to force labor and management to make decisions they would not otherwise have made. Consider the difficulties in applying such a policy. The government has to know what the appropriate price should be and how it should change over time. Suppose, for example, that the government had set a target rate of inflation of 4 percent. Does this mean that all prices should be rising by 4 percent? Not at all. If there is any real growth going on in the economy, some products are expanding. Even in the absence of any greater than normal price increases in the raw material costs or wages, prices may rise in the industry because of diminishing returns. How much they rise depends on just how hard it is to expand output. In a growing economy the demand for different products grows at different rates, and the ability to supply that increased demand varies with industries. The government would have to know each industry's supply curve to determine the justifiable price increase it should be granted. Another problem immediately comes to mind. What signal does the market have for raising output other than profits? If demand rises in an industry, prices are raised, profits increase, and business in that industry is prompted to expand its facilities and to increase its output. The short-run rise in prices is the legitimate signaling device of the market economy by which more output will later be supplied. If the government short-circuits the signal, no extra output will be forthcoming. This is all right if government sets the right price. If it sets one that is too low, the substitute for inflation is a smaller total output and perhaps rationing. One sees examples of this in public utilities and cities with rent controls. Prices set at artifically low levels have created long-run shortages in electric power, natural gas, and housing.

When people talk about wage and price guidelines, they generally seem to be talking about monitoring the giant industries—steel, automobiles, chemical, and others. But this sector may not be the principal cause of the inflation of consumer prices at all. Examine the consumer price index. The kinds of things that are important—rent, haircuts, auto repairs, laundry, medical services, and food—are not provided by the giant industries. Edwin L. Dale put it well in *The Nation* when he wrote:

> Let us, as a starter, take up some real-world examples that have a lot more to do with the cost of living than the sort of thing these plans have in mind—say, whether the United States Steel Company raises the price of hot rolled sheets.
>
> The Mothers of Mercy hospital in Peoria raises its rate for a room from $40 to $50 a day. Is the President's Council of Economic Advisers supposed to intervene?
>
> Fred Richards Auto Body Shop raises the charge for fixing a fender in Richmond from $20 to $30. Is President Nixon to call Fred Richards to the White House?
>
> There is a freeze in Florida and the price of orange juice goes up, raising the month's consumer price index by one-tenth of one percent all by itself. Does the Attorney General bring an antitrust suit against the orange growers?
>
> The Washington Senators raise the price of seats to the ball game—also in the index. Does the President announce that he will go to no more ball games?[1]

It is inconceivable that any government, however well intentioned or well informed, could keep track of the many millions of local price decisions which determine how the cost of living actually rises for any one of us. Wage and price guideposts may successfully prevent a highly visible industry such as steel from raising its prices, as happened in 1962, but one suspects that such action will only delay the higher prices, not prevent them. Furthermore, it may make the industry so relatively unprofitable that it is incapable of attracting the capital to modernize and expand its facilities.

---

[1] Edwin L. Dale, Jr. "Jawboning's a Joke," *The New Republic* (April 18, 1970).

If you say to the public that the inflation control program consists of stopping "excessive" wage and price increases in the automobile or the steel industry, people are going to believe that it is those excessive price and wage increases that caused the inflation. That is not true. In the last analysis, inflations are caused by excess demand, which often results from government deficit spending. A good deal of the inflation may occur after the original excess demand is eliminated, but only because perception of inflation and reactions to it are not instantaneous. Inflation is a process, as we have insisted, that works itself out over time in response to an initial stimulus. One should not be fooled into forgetting that—just because prices continue to rise after excess demand disappears during the stabilization phase. Are we advocating a do-nothing policy for the government? No, we are merely asking the government to stop initiating inflations through unfinanced spending programs when the economy is at full employment.

In the final analysis the success of any stabilization program depends on the patience and understanding of the electorate. It has to understand the connection between today's idle capacity and yesterday's boom. It must be willing to accept a longer period of inflationary stagnation the longer the preceding inflation was allowed to continue. Keynesian economics has taught us how to control the level of our national income and how to avoid depressions. But it has not taught us any way that we can permanently force our economy to more than capacity output and employment without ever-accelerating inflation. We have found to our sorrow that there is no trade-off between inflation and employment, that the long-run willingness of labor to work and its productivity are the final determinants of full employment price and output. Inflation obscures these realities only in the short run.

Questions

1. Throughout this book, we have characterized inflation as a more or less short-run phenomenon. Yet some countries,

such as Chile, have experienced continuous and high rates of inflation for decades. Can such an apparent paradox be explained within the framework of the theory presented?

2. Is "jawboning a joke"? That is, can you think of any circumstances where such a policy might be warranted?

3. Are there circumstances where wage or price controls might be warranted?

4. Would cost of living escalator clauses be inflationary?

5. Is taxation as an anti-inflationary tool doomed to practical ineffectiveness as a result of the remarkable time lag between the need for the tax and the passage of the tax law? Do you have any recommendations about how the time lag can be shortened?

6. In 1962 President John F. Kennedy prevented the steel industry from raising its prices. Was this action anti-inflationary? Is there a difference between the short-run and the long run effects of the policy?

7. Suppose you were going to institute a system of price controls. Would you allow any price increases? Would you make exceptions for firms that are increasing their output? How would you decide the "right" price for each industry?

Suggestions for Further Reading

Galbraith, John K., "Market Structure and Stabilization Policy," *Review of Economics and Statistics* (May 1957), 124–133.

Schultz, G. P., and R. Z. Aliber, eds., *Guidelines, Informal Controls and the Market Place.* Chicago: University of Chicago Press, 1966.

Smithies, Arthur, "The Control of Inflation," *Review of Economics and Statistics* (August 1957), 272–283.

Ullman, Lloyd, "Under Severe Restraint: British Incomes Policy," *Industrial Relations* (May 1967), 213–266.

Weintraub, Sidney, "A Proposal to Halt the Spiral of Wages and Prices," *New York Times*, November 29, 1970.

A
APPENDIX

Tables

TABLE A.1 Prices, 1950–1970 (1967 = 100)

Consumer Price Indexes, by Major Groups

Year	All Items	Food	Housing Total	Housing Rent	Apparel and Upkeep	Transportation	Medical Care	Personal Care	Reading and Recreation	Other Goods and Services	Wholesale Price Index
1950	72.1	74.5	72.8	70.4	79.0	68.2	53.7	68.3	74.4	69.9	81.8
1951	77.8	82.8	77.2	73.2	86.1	72.5	56.3	74.7	76.6	72.8	91.1
1952	79.5	84.3	78.7	76.2	85.3	77.3	59.3	75.6	76.9	76.6	88.6
1953	80.1	83.0	80.8	80.3	84.6	79.5	61.4	76.3	77.7	78.5	87.4
1954	80.5	82.8	81.7	83.2	84.5	78.3	63.4	76.6	76.9	79.8	87.6
1955	80.2	81.6	82.3	84.3	84.1	77.4	64.8	77.9	76.7	79.8	87.8
1956	81.4	82.2	83.6	85.9	85.8	78.8	67.2	81.1	77.8	81.0	90.7
1957	84.3	84.9	86.2	87.5	87.3	83.3	69.9	84.1	80.7	83.3	93.3
1958	86.6	88.5	87.7	89.1	87.5	86.0	73.2	86.9	83.9	84.4	94.6
1959	87.3	87.1	88.6	90.4	88.2	89.6	76.4	88.7	85.3	86.1	94.8
1960	88.7	88.0	90.2	91.7	89.6	89.6	79.1	90.1	87.3	87.8	94.9
1961	89.6	89.1	90.9	92.9	90.4	90.6	81.4	90.6	89.3	88.5	94.5
1962	90.6	89.9	91.7	94.0	90.9	92.5	83.5	92.2	91.3	89.1	94.8
1963	91.7	91.2	92.7	95.0	91.9	93.0	85.6	93.4	92.8	90.6	94.5
1964	92.9	92.4	93.8	95.9	92.7	94.3	87.3	94.5	95.0	92.0	94.7
1965	94.5	94.4	94.9	96.9	93.7	95.9	89.5	95.2	95.9	94.2	96.6
1966	97.2	99.1	97.2	98.2	96.1	97.2	93.4	97.1	97.5	97.2	99.8
1967	100.0	100.0	100.0	100.0	100.0	100.0	100.0	100.0	100.0	100.0	100.0
1968	104.2	103.6	104.2	102.4	105.4	103.2	106.1	104.2	104.7	104.6	102.5
1969	109.8	108.9	110.8	105.7	111.5	107.2	113.4	109.3	108.7	109.1	106.5
1970	116.1	114.9	118.6	109.8	115.8	112.3	120.3	113.0	113.1	115.7	110.4

SOURCE: *Economic Report of the President, 1971*. (The source for all the tables in Appendix A is the *Economic Report*.)

143

TABLE A.2

Rates of Inflation, 1950–1970
(annual percentage changes)

Year	Consumer Price Index	Wholesale Price Index
1950	1.0	3.9
1951	7.9	11.4
1952	2.2	−2.7
1953	0.8	−1.4
1954	0.5	0.2
1955	−0.4	0.2
1956	1.5	3.3
1957	3.6	2.9
1958	2.7	1.4
1959	0.8	0.2
1960	1.6	0.1
1961	1.0	−0.4
1962	1.1	0.3
1963	1.2	−0.3
1964	1.3	0.2
1965	1.7	2.0
1966	2.9	3.3
1967	2.8	0.2
1968	4.2	2.5
1969	5.4	3.9
1970	5.7	3.7

TABLE A.3   National Accounts, 1950–1970   (billions of dollars, 1958 prices)

Year	GNP	Disposable Personal Income	Personal Consumption	Private Domestic Investment	Government Expenditures on Goods and Services		Exports	Imports
					Federal	State & Local		
1950	355.3	249.6	230.5	69.3	25.3	27.5	16.3	13.6
1951	383.4	255.7	232.8	70.0	47.4	27.9	19.3	14.1
1952	395.1	263.3	239.4	60.5	63.8	28.4	18.2	15.2
1953	412.8	275.4	250.8	61.2	70.0	29.7	17.8	16.7
1954	407.0	278.3	255.7	59.4	56.8	32.1	18.8	15.8
1955	438.0	296.7	274.2	75.4	50.7	34.4	20.9	17.7
1956	446.1	309.3	281.4	74.3	49.7	35.6	24.2	19.1
1957	452.5	315.8	288.2	68.8	51.7	37.6	26.2	19.9
1958	447.3	318.8	290.1	60.9	53.6	40.6	23.1	20.9
1959	475.9	333.0	307.3	73.6	52.5	42.2	23.8	23.5
1960	487.7	340.2	316.1	72.4	51.4	43.5	27.3	23.0
1961	497.2	350.7	322.5	69.0	54.6	45.9	28.0	22.9
1962	529.8	367.3	338.4	79.4	60.0	47.5	30.0	25.5
1963	551.0	381.3	353.3	82.5	59.5	50.1	32.1	26.6
1964	581.1	407.9	373.7	87.8	58.1	53.2	36.5	28.2
1965	617.8	435.0	397.7	99.2	57.9	56.8	37.4	31.2
1966	658.1	458.9	418.1	109.3	65.4	61.1	40.2	36.1
1967	675.2	477.5	430.1	101.2	74.7	65.5	42.1	38.5
1968	707.2	499.0	452.3	105.7	78.7	69.6	45.7	44.8
1969	727.1	511.5	467.7	111.3	75.7	72.1	48.5	48.2
1970	724.3	529.7	477.2	103.0	67.7	74.1	52.2	49.9

TABLE A.4

Labor Market Data

Year	Unemployment Rates (workers)	Real Wages*	Index of Labor Cost Sales 1967 = 100
1950	5.3%	$ 80.89	137.1
1951	3.3	81.41	129.0
1952	3.0	84.48	129.5
1953	2.9	87.98	129.0
1954	5.5	87.57	134.2
1955	4.4	94.39	128.1
1956	4.1	96.78	130.3
1957	4.3	96.79	130.5
1958	6.8	95.51	134.1
1959	5.5	101.10	128.2
1960	5.5	101.15	127.3
1961	6.7	103.06	127.5
1962	5.5	106.58	121.0
1963	5.7	108.65	117.4
1964	5.2	110.84	112.4
1965	4.5	113.79	106.5
1966	3.8	115.58	100.6
1967	3.8	114.90	100.0
1968	3.6	117.57	97.0
1969	3.5	117.95	94.8
1970	4.9	115.19	96.3

* Average gross weekly earnings, 1967 prices.

TABLE A.5

Factor Shares, 1950–1970

Year	Total Wage Income as a Percent of National Income	Corporation Profits Before Taxes as a Percent of National Income*
1950	64.1%	15.6%
1951	65.0	15.4
1952	67.0	13.7
1953	68.6	13.0
1954	68.6	12.5
1955	67.8	14.2
1956	69.3	13.1
1957	69.9	12.5
1958	70.1	11.2
1959	69.8	12.9
1960	71.0	12.0
1961	70.8	11.8
1962	70.7	12.2
1963	70.8	12.2
1964	70.6	12.8
1965	69.8	13.5
1966	70.2	13.3
1967	71.5	12.0
1968	72.1	12.0
1969	73.3	11.2
1970	74.9	9.7

* Includes inventory valuation adjustment.

TABLE A.6

Fiscal and Monetary Data

Year	Money Supply* (billions of dollars, 1958 prices)	Federal Government Receipts as a Percent of GNP	State and Local Government Receipts as a Percent of GNP
1950	133.4	17.5%	7.4%
1951	133.1	19.5	7.1
1952	137.0	19.5	7.3
1953	137.6	19.2	7.5
1954	142.0	17.5	7.9
1955	144.6	18.1	7.9
1956	142.3	18.5	8.3
1957	137.1	18.5	8.7
1958	140.0	17.6	9.3
1959	139.4	18.5	9.5
1960	136.4	19.2	9.9
1961	139.7	18.9	10.3
1962	140.0	19.0	10.5
1963	142.8	19.4	10.7
1964	147.5	18.2	11.0
1965	151.4	18.2	11.0
1966	149.7	19.0	11.4
1967	154.9	19.0	11.8
1968	159.6	20.3	12.3
1969	155.1	21.5	12.7
1970	154.9	20.0	13.6

* Average December currency supply plus demand deposits divided by December CPI, 1958 = 100.

TABLE A.7

Balance of Payments, 1950–1970
(millions of current dollars)

Year	Balance on Goods and Services (1)	Net Capital Flows, Pensions, Remittances, and Unrecorded Transactions (2)	Liquidity Balance (3) = (1) + (2)
1950	1,892	−5,381	−3,489
1951	3,817	−3,825	−8
1952	2,356	−3,562	−1,206
1953	532	−2,716	−2,184
1954	1,959	−3,500	−1,541
1955	2,153	−3,395	−1,242
1956	4,145	−5,118	−973
1957	5,901	−5,323	578
1958	2,356	−5,721	−3,365
1959	310	−4,180	−3,870
1960	4,133	−8,034	−3,901
1961	5,622	−7,993	−2,371
1962	5,149	−7,353	−2,204
1963	5,984	−8,654	−2,670
1964	8,580	−11,380	−2,800
1965	7,121	−8,456	−1,335
1966	5,300	−6,657	−1,357
1967	5,213	−8,757	−3,544
1968	2,493	−2,322	171
1969	1,949	−8,961	−7,012
1970	3,943	−9,426	−4,415*

* Includes allocation of special drawing rights.

TABLE A.8

International Consumer Price Indexes, 1957–1970
(1963 = 100)

Year	United States	Canada	Japan	France	Germany	Italy	Netherlands	United Kingdom
1957	91.8	91.7	79.3	69.6	88.1	83.2	88	86.9
1958	94.4	94.1	78.9	80.1	90.0	85.5	90	89.5
1959	95.1	95.1	79.8	85.0	90.9	85.1	91	90.0
1960	96.6	96.2	82.6	88.1	92.1	87.1	94	90.9
1961	97.7	97.1	87.0	91.0	94.3	88.9	95	94.0
1962	98.8	98.3	93.0	95.4	97.1	93.1	97	98.0
1963	100.0	100.0	100.0	100.0	100.0	100.0	100	100.0
1964	101.3	101.8	103.9	103.4	102.3	105.9	106	103.3
1965	103.0	104.3	110.7	106.0	105.8	110.7	111.0	108.2
1966	106.0	108.2	116.4	108.9	109.5	113.3	117.4	112.4
1967	109.0	112.0	121.0	111.8	111.1	116.9	121.4	115.2
1968	113.6	116.7	127.5	116.9	113.1	118.5	125.9	120.6
1969	119.7	122.0	134.1	124.4	116.1	121.6	135.3	127.2
1970	126.5	126.0	143.5	130.5	120.2	126.9	140.7	134.5

B
APPENDIX

Readings on Inflation and Economic Development

Baer, Werner, "The Inflation Controversy in Latin America: A Survey," *Latin American Research Review* (Spring 1967), 3-25.

————, "Brazil: Inflation and Economic Efficiency," *Economic Development and Cultural Change* (July 1963), 395–406. Werner Baer and Isaac Kerstenetsky, eds.

———— and Isaac Kerstenetzky, Inflation and Growth in Latin America. Homewood, Ill.: Irwin, 1964.

Bernstein, E. M., and I. G. Patec, "Inflation in Relation to Economic Development," *IMF Staff Papers* (November 1952), 363–398.

Dorrance, G. S., "The Effect of Inflation on Economic Development," *IMF Staff Papers* (March 1963), 1–47.

Economic Commission for Latin America, "Inflation and Growth: A Summary of Experience in Latin America," *Economic Bulletin for Latin America* (February 1962).

Harburger, Arnold, "The Dynamics of Inflation in Chile" in Carl Christ et al. *Measurement in Economics.* Stanford: Calif.: Stanford University Press, 1963.

Kaldor, Nicholas, "Economic Growth and the Problem of Inflation," *Economica*, Pt. I-II (August and November 1959). 212–226, 287–298.

Maynard, Geoffrey, *Economic Development and the Price Level*. London: Macmillan & Company, 1963.

————, "Inflation and Growth: Some Lessons to be Drawn from the Latin American Experience," *Oxford Economic Papers* (June 1961), 184–202.

Morley, Samuel A., "Inflation and Stagnation in Brazil," *Economic Development and Cultural Change* (January 1971), 184–203.

National Council of Applied Economic Research, *Growth without Inflation* (Sidney Weintraub, au.). New Delhi, India, 1965. (New York: International Publications Service).

Seers, Dudley, "A Theory of Inflation and Growth in Underdeveloped Economies Based on the Experience of Latin America," *Oxford Economic Papers* (June 1962), 173–195.